Édouard Glissant

A New Region of the World: Aesthetics I

THE GLISSANT TRANSLATION PROJECT

Édouard Glissant

A New Region of the World: Aesthetics I

translated by
Martin Munro

LIVERPOOL UNIVERSITY PRESS

First published 2023 by
Liverpool University Press
4 Cambridge Street
Liverpool
L69 7ZU

This paperback edition published 2024

UNE NOUVELLE RÉGION DU MONDE
Esthétique I
© Editions Gallimard, 2006

Martin Munro has asserted the right to be identified as the translator of this
book in accordance with the Copyright, Designs and Patents Act 1988.

British Library Cataloguing-in-Publication data
A British Library CIP record is available

ISBN 978-1-80207-796-4 hardback
ISBN 978-1-80207-797-1 softback

Typeset by Carnegie Book Production, Lancaster
Printed and bound by CPI Group (UK) Ltd, Croydon CR0 4YY

We shall meet where the oceans join…

Contents

IN THE SPACE OF A DAY, THE VOICES
SPREAD LIKE SEA FOAM, SO THAT
THEY TOUCH THESE CENTURIES
THAT CLING TO THE DIAMANT ROCK,
AND FROM WHICH SWIRL MULTIPLE
CHAOS-OPERAS.

The gateway to the sea, purple and blue and violet, raises with a single wave what grows gradually in the black depths, and this vivid alliance of light and darkness, *they allocated me the light, and I lived in the dark*, and then this strike of a baroque and difficult and grainy blade, it thrusts in turns like the weft of a text. What did we expect from this trip so strictly limited to the confines of the bay? We believe that the rock is a point of recovery or rallying, and that it has survived the brutal collapse of the crest of the hills that once jutted into the water like a rudder oar, and between it and the land there is now a pass crossed by devious currents and malignant winds which disguise themselves under the ruses of the sun. The English navy took advantage of it two centuries ago to establish a stockade there, two batteries of cannons, a hospital, and a gunpowder mill on the rock: this extreme point had become a bastion of war, a real, all-powerful ship at anchor. You find almost everywhere, on the tormented or calm coastlines of seas and oceans these same signs of exclamation or interrogation, made of tangled cliffs and cut out in chalky laces, or gentle hills with red grasses sprouting and forests cut to the ground. For us here it is the good Larcher Hill populated with its snakes, and with staves of smooth and weary alluvium flowing into the water like sunburned lizards, and which all end abruptly or quietly in the wave that cuts like a channel or passage or abyss or leviathan, either in the seas of the deserts or in the furious oceans, and these hills and these cliffs and these esplanades of sand or mud all tend toward the point that was once their absolute extremity. Such a repetition of the motif—the storms strike and sculpt everywhere in the same way—makes visible there the emerging shape of one or more hidden meanings. The continental part of this figure establishes for us the present of things, the net of realities, that which is ephemeral or that changes. The curve barely glimpsed under the water, the terrain of the collapse that happened a long time ago, perpetuates the concordance of the past in this present, or suggests in big-big bubbles the continuities of the underwater lavas gushing from the surrounding living or dead volcanoes that blend their fires below, and to finish here is the rock (the point), which is in itself an old archipelago, so irreducible in its sculpted fragility. The muffled mornings and the evaporated nights hollow it out and eat at it without drying it up, and it maintains the link, questioning or exclaiming, and it throws worry and wonder through the whole structure, which seizes you, like a rolling tide, everything is clear and legible, and this point, pockmarked cape or peak or arch devoted to the whistling winds or double chimney planted with clouds, or needle stitching its mists, consecrates in front of you and wherever it might be in the world, and so do you, the same land-sea sign, of cays carried early far away and inaccessible obscurities rising from the bottom, and which strengthens and carries your outcry. Sinking then into the chaos of signs, before slowly finding itself in the clarity or density of a meaning. The Rock rises on the slopes of the waters.

Exclamation and interrogation exalt that which has spread over the entire surface of the land that leads to the coast, they thus sum up a human advance and the meditation that followed it, so pensive, the body leaning forward and the arms crossed under the armpits as if to better understand the sign that appears, you would say that all the powers of the winds and the waters and the friable heat and the brittle cold that have shaped this whole, the same across the world, were also to announce the arrival of a contemplator, who interrogates here or who exclaims there. Yet it is the sea that matters, it fills the smashed bubble-hole, between the mass of the figure and its full stop (the rock), with a question or an exclamation more evasive and at the same time more pointed, how does the beauty of this place here correspond with so much blue randomness to the beauty of that place there which is so like it and that one finds in the saline vegetation of Brazil or in the worst Breton sea sprays or the cleanly cut capes of Tierra del Fuego, or to the thickness of the lacquered burials of Norway or in the barely visible edges of the snow and ice of the Siberian coasts, in other words, what is beauty, which thus ranges from the pulverulent to the frangible and to violence and meditation and far away and just below?

And what is beauty, which travels across so many of these repetitions, the same bodies of earth and rocks, which advance in this purple-blue-violet or this briny dew or this yellowed silt of river mouths, with then the same fault lines in the matter and so much fury of winds and seas piled up in their movements, and these end points, blindly the same, rocks or bare peaks or stalagmites or styluses or lagoons, or else this fullness of sea foam that you see at the end of the continents tapered to infinity, cursed cape, or cape of hope, where you meet not one but an infinity of points of declination, punctuation marks of rocks whose perforated masses dwindle in proportion and which beat the sea foam, at this time like immaterial suspension points, and here the Diamant Rock! What is beauty, along the lakes and the backwaters, and in the sands of retreating seas and at the tip of the canes and in the gullies of snow and on the crazy sidewalks of drifting cities? And again, in the unified voices and birthing gestures and high arches, these infinite points of interrogation and exclamation which find in us their seas and their shores. Everywhere in the world, this extreme point is set up, hermitage and temple and lazaretto and fortified castle and large market towns launching their sloped streets and their stalls that form walls and gentle camouflaged churches and cathedrals which reign high on their fields of seaweed and their cloisters with no exit other than the infinity of a sky and the small lighthouses installed there as if playing at riddles of light and very, very far away these caves at the end of a climbing rope, where anchorites with braided beards turn to stone, or quite simply land sown with para grass where troops of wild sheep are united, the humanities and their aspects in these places of passage between land and water are always held at the extreme of their lives, and here again, and right-here again, the Diamant Rock. We observe that the body of earth which thus projects toward its fall or its conclusion is of a reclining lady, the chin is very determined and the nose strong and raised, the Rock behind is like the top of a comb hanging on some plait of underwater hair. One of our joyful friends claims that it is instead the unhooded glans of a huge penis that the lady is stroking from below, furtively. It is in truth the sea that dominates, and as soon as the sand leaves it has mixed up the meshes of the text that it deciphers, which makes it that from the shore to the edges of the Rock the reading is more difficult and the depth unfathomable and you cannot follow the unfolding of the knots and articulations, and the approaches to what you still do not know to be this beauty are surely forbidden to you and you will have to suffer to find this beauty and the sections of text have become enclosed without you being able to cling to anything coherent, the thing has changed from before, and nothing more is readable, the seas are inconstant and fatal, it is a shared place, are you going to die there, alone and inspired, so close to this shore, in a mass of unstable jetsam? Paddle hard, soon the long grasses, or whatever has taken their place, move aside, and you imagine *Sargassum* and slave ships as becalmed as the caravels of Columbus and you see the *Santa-Maria* and the three-masted slave vessels engulfing off the coasts of the archipelago and you go around the Rock and you see the ruins and here you see that the side that faces the open sea is high and wild like a face without expression so you watch there the birds massing in the dark of the highest crevasses and the seabeds rise permeable and you stammer what you do not know to be a true aesthetic prediction, thus in so many places of the world where beauty appears no one would think that they could have established an activity and a thought and a fire and a concern and a law and a desire which in the end would be predictions of aesthetics, and which an aesthetic could therefore proclaim, it is the power of being displaced by rocks and earth and water and foam in the form of questions and exclamations, or rather the infinite suspension that this displacement makes when it clings to the mad words and serene matters of art, or perhaps a cry once again, all this aesthetics, all these aesthetics, that you do not distinguish from one another, whose geographies you do not see spread around so many seas, *it's a cry that breathes in fresh air* once again from our sparks in the bush, and with blueish lianas and rainbow algae, and always in such places, advances in infinity, the cries fall in tangles and start again forms of chaos.

So here you consult all those polished and lustered river rocks that have rushed to meet the big jagged chunks of rocks and cold lava, and around the Rock, itself in pieces but all as one and its hollows like eyes of the night or mouths of shadow and its protrusions like dried up dismantled noses, and from the shore up to here, you consider how the initially confused word has mingled with gray sands—the words are stiff and left on the page—and has been clarified by a cartage of great auspicious darkness and has been made clear by an infinity of those senses that all tremble there, the words then lapped the rock like fresh water. It is in really fine weather the word of the cays that catch the wind and watch over the reefs.

Obscure *Langages**

---

*   To begin to explain how Glissant thinks about language, I cite Michael
Wiedorn's glossary for his translation of *Philosophy of Relation*: "English has one
word, 'language,' French boasts two: *'langue'* and *'langage.'* In broad terms, the
first (*'langue'*) refers to particular tongues, as in 'the English language.' *'Langage,'*
however, is both more general and more fundamental, appearing in such phrasings
as 'a computer programming language' or 'body language' in French. In a telling
remark, Glissant points out that Caribbean writers who speak different languages
(*'langues'*) can nonetheless express themselves in the same language (*'langage'*)." In
this translation, I will use "language" for "*langues*" and retain *langage*.

MONDE MUNDUS MONDO MUNDO MOUNE, AND TIMOUNE, AND IN ALL THE LANGUAGES, ALIVE AND DEAD AND UNBORN, AND IN SOME OTHERS STILL.

The most grounded certainties, when the dive into certainties happens to encounter a bottom, say that we are all now entering into *a new region of the world*, which designates its sites on all the given and imaginable expanses, and of which only a few had been able to foresee in the distance its wanderings and obscurities. We believe that these foreshadowing wanderings, these foretelling obscurities, if they present themselves still today in overly apocalyptic contexts, would be no less propitious for a renewed energy of the matter of the world, or for a means of regeneration, as all the inaugural catastrophes appear to be, memories of a dizzying creation and whose varieties are difficult to foretell. We must underline the contrasts (the gaps) between the colorations (which are so many nuances) of what we would call the landscapes of the world, and then return to our general tonalities of existence and ask ourselves if these tonalities are in mutual harmony, mixing the deep colors of these landscapes, or if they persist in a lonely desperate monotony (assuming monotony to be every time a negation), or if they open up for us new possibilities and renewed exaltations and a very unexpected recommencement, in countries finally reunited. If you approach the obscure problems that the humanities face, you will reduce them one by one, clearly and distinctly, but if they multiply ad infinitum then you will not be able to conceive of their totality nor be moved by it, which knows no limits, and all your resolutions will fall and your all too frail clarities will shatter one against the other, and then we will not be able to frequent this totality nor finally hope to really come together in it if we do not accumulate differences and relationships of differences, these elements of relation between all things known and unknown, of course resemblance is futile and difference pulsates, and that as elements we have so long failed to recognize, but which enable us to endure the coarse thicknesses of diversities in order then to reveal to ourselves finally reconciliations of meaning and radiances, so tranquil. And we will have to get used to the fact that meaning sometimes does not manifest *one-single* transparency nor any kind of clarity, and to think or feel our way within such a complexity. Here is what would be the treatise on difference that would sum up in mumbo-jumbo whatever aesthetic there may be. Thus, a leap into the unknown and the obscure, before the text could become clear, or go from any clarity to any form of the unexpected, and which will follow the same uncertain cascading course down to the Rock. A single day filled the entire space of the world. Any such aesthetic, and even though it is only a matter of exercising the most intolerant rules of a rhetoric, was first decided based on inextricable impenetrable naked masses, and on very bright lights and very hard foliage, and colors and echoes, the softness of which however sometimes deviates, and in which it was not easy to extricate any meaning. Aesthetics have always made their object more and more complex, before shedding light on it. The masses of techniques add their unfathomable pulverescence to it.

The same gaps have opened up in all of these conceivable forms of *we*. Let us be aware that the distribution of these forms of we sometimes extends over the flight of a butterfly. We followed frantically the trails of this butterfly, between hurricanes and earthquakes. We stigmatize the colors of these we, which we also claim, and whose nuances lead to so many reasons to *distinguish*, however coarsely that may be done. What is this we, otherwise so quotidian? What is this we that doubts here, and with what does it resound? It has extended multiply at the same time as our so-called *new region of the world* has expanded. And every time, that extension has been assembled on the same scale as the rapid flow of understanding. We say *all of we*. And the more we are in saying this, the less sure we are of what it means. Let us please think of this we rising there, whole but obscured. Will it bring together as many fakers as makers of memory, who yesterday opposed or fought one another so much, as well as those who believe the world to be a passage as much as those who reject this from the depths of their terrors of old, and those who have benefited as much as those who have run dry? This region itself, we soon foresee, as difficult as it may seem to formulate its partition, is mixed in time as much as in space, a common site which hides another gap. Time has changed and space has changed. A steep separation of time and space, overwhelming each other. A new region that is an epoch, mixing all times and all durations, an epoch also which is an inexhaustible country, accumulating expanses, which are looking for other limits, in incalculable but always finite number, as has been said of atoms. There, extreme confusion of times and spaces of this notion of here, which moves closer to a new country of which we know nothing and into which we will enter. Humanities do not get the measure of these geographies of today and we more readily imagine being hemmed in by borders which appear immeasurable. For a long time we have been seeking to understand how the differences have grown there between the nuances of things and the shades of the countries and their monotony, and on the other hand in us the voices and the ideas and the fury and the passion and the rumination, and the floods.

Try in your turn to listen to the privileged few who had sensed the obscurities of the world, privilege was of no use or benefit to them, only the cachet of their small number, and in the chaos of the torments of this world they could not be heard, they had no way of accommodating one idea rather than another nor a nude color rather than one that would be draped or embellished nor to lighten or reinforce these new colors, they were content to be so well installed in the ranks of the amiable and the entertainers, they secretly admired the change makers, or those who were reputed as such, men of action and shareholders, those who weigh gold and silver, the fine measurers of death. In the change now so total of the world, and which had changed from its first palpitation, no change could any longer be considered decisive or even to be assuredly active. What we would have imagined to be the youth or the renewed energy of this world was in the end the meeting of all that is ancient in it, which, for once united, considered itself together. And the youth of the world, this was indeed the conjunction of so many primordial diversities, radically aged, which by all joining together became obsessed with each other, knowing each other were so mutually innocent. The feelings of the obscurities grown from their encounters, and predicted by some, were of little use. The breach opened by these clashes of diversities had not left us the leisure to turn our heads and look back. Neither Rimbaud, nor Chaka Zoulou, Nadja, Nedjma, Colino who beat Fort-de-France, the Intruder in the dust and nor the one who lived in the explosion and neither Maldoror who suffered the old parting of the water, nor papa Longoué nor Diogène nor that enigmatic Queen of Madagascar. Fanon nor the Rebel. In us, there was nothing that bore the trace nor the remains of a treaty of the Apocalypse, of a gift nor of a cry of prophecy.

Consider these predictions, they are above all the announcements of an intuition, and *after all* constitutive of reality, and thus the privilege of these obscure announcers of the living obscurity of the Whole-World, and of these cursed poets, of these so frenzied storytellers, and of these visionary philosophers and of these sagacious peoples, betrayed people, people stiffened under the whip and the baton, it was good to be in the world in the manner of intuitive bodies, which were neither heard nor understood, but well and truly allusive, who thus were free to wander the world, and who in the end predicted its reality. The undeclared privilege of these philosophers and poets and griots and street criers. It was realized that, in order to finally extinguish their noise, both individually and in general, the best common and bearable way to endure the unstoppable change (of everything) was to take it wholly as an entertainment, which was facilitated or suggested by the fabulous techniques, dear to the wealthy countries of the world. The thinkers had solemnly declared a becoming-world, the audiences enjoyed the spectacle, greatly enlarged by the prowess of these techniques. In the places where science had advanced, it was supposed, with great balances of dramatic contradictions, and very often kept secret before their resolutions were recognized and proclaimed, the techniques themselves grew by pleasant accumulations, and immediately made public, and *applied* to the maximum possible, and very soon they served to divert us from most of the convulsions of the world, *even if* the convulsions took place at the heart of their disturbances. We quickly got used to these diversions, and now we watch them go by. The peoples become the audiences. And you will have a hard time stacking up the greenhouse effects and the melting of the poles and the universal silica of the forests and the exterminations of the peoples and the widespread tortures, tortures finally wandering in the air, and the extinctions of children and all those varieties of common places. The more you tilt your head, and the less you hear of the coming day, and if you look up you do not see the *banyan of the rain*. Space and time make a single cinema where you roam and gape. So many misfortunes, fixed and frozen in the very powerful weight of their single representation are, as soon as signaled, diverted. No forecast, even if it arises from an intuition, either prevails or guides. Our news, for all that it comes from the real events of the world, torments us severely.

Recall, thanks to interpretations of colors and shades and monotony of hues, in the way of fashion makers, or to the overgrown bush that firefighters combat, or to the drying up of words, worse than the salt marshes or the stinking marshes watched over by the beach cleaners, that which is passion or judgment or anger, or decline, the permanent disputes of the body and the mind, is this a legitimate transfer? Why keep the gap between such categories so wide, and still suppose that it is growing? *This is because these are the countries that prevail.* As we have seen what the seas do. Countries change us. The countries, the landscapes. The words we have used mystify their material. Cause and effect are of little use, we will have to get used to differences in causes which would produce different effects. And the smelters fill the pounds, the golden palm trees uproot the sands, the gray suburbs shoot up in the mirrored districts. It rots fig mats in the recesses of the night. All through that same hard night, the factories have taken their stake. A few determined researchers have made a starry light. New. Nuclear, no doubt. Suddenly, bulk sales, in the shadow of a highway. Repetition, banal, echo, echo, abstractly. But to speak, tireless, and to repeat, to accumulate. Volcanoes and cyclones do not discern. When floods and fires take turns blindly. Water the fire. Earth. The clouds by tens of thousands, the dead by tens of millions. And your passions your whirlwinds. Which keep turning over. *Because it is the landscapes that chant.* The heavy and muffled tremors of the city. The minimal soul trade, banal quotidian. And the time that overtakes. Where it is how many generations for a small-small result of proven synthesis, five, ten, so few, but nowadays only one maybe. Thought goes slower than and not so far as speed, which dazzles. The speed of what? Of chaos. We expand our imaginations and create other ways of knowing and relating. We become limpid, and so peaceful, in the whirlwind. Here it is no longer but cloud, and there a bottomless opera. Disentangled.

The world thus, its disputes and struggles, do we then see it as a painting, or as a representation? Let us ask this with gravity, but without further delay, because we believe in the power of these figurations. The painting endures and it perpetuates and freezes a moment, even when it designates the pure moving, either a battle or a flowing stream or the beginning of a sadness, and the representation *unfolds*, even when it takes a long time to *exhibit*. These are two of the effects of meditation and action. And there are of course lopsided universes, that are to tell the truth without will or desire for an autonomous representation and without any possible production of a painting distinguished from the surrounding thing, but they express the fixity or the movement of the relation to their surroundings in other ways we will get to. At times in their histories, other humanities, resolutely on the move, producers of paintings and of representations, caught on to the play of differences, but it was to deny them absolutely, and to found the identical. We undertake this poetry with three, perhaps motionless, steps: the appearance, under the transparent awning of the calamities, of a so-called *new region of the world*; the perceivable force of the colors of the landscapes; and namely, in third and true place, if that inaugurates a light, a white or a black or of any shade that may come, or that rather sends us into another deleterious confusion. Poetry is assembled, from those faceted parts of words, which clearly say that the book will not go in one block nor in a single caravan. The book is obliged, like any painting or representation, to take and catch the moment in its motion. Language transmutes, it decides or inclines. At all these moments, language risks modifying the rootedness of things, the volatile sentiment we have of them, and diverting the crowd from our rites and our stories. Namely, language draws and colors first, *and then recites*. We end up understanding that we are at the crossroads where have reached peoples who have aimed far and peoples who have looked toward the earth. The picture, the painted picture, is on the contrary an isolate, a halt, a quotation of details, from which one freely selects the detail, and it is too bad for the enlightening synthesis and the golden number and the unanimous structure, too bad for the *unseen* history and for the unknown evolution of this series of paintings, that is to say of painting, which we will come back to. We must stay for the moment with the intention of all this devolution, look then, with his painting the artist wanted, in the continents and across the archipelagos, on marble, buildings, pieces of wood, easels, canvas, bare bones, torn doors, *to fix* a story in a region of time and of space, the painting was a language that recited before formulating or coloring, but soon this same painting, recommenced millions of times, set out, in our time, on a more autonomous route, and almost outside of the deliberation of painters and blacksmiths, sacred or cursed, to enter openly into the chaos of being! Then the painting as if by itself tensed up to tell the story of this chaos, and how this kind of painting had slipped from the former taking possession of the real to an attempt to merge with it, an old, immoderate, and quite frankly original ambition, and how this sort of representation, which sometimes was inscribed equally well in words and songs, had wanted to pass from the naked imitation of the real to the assumption of all its materials (of all the possible surroundings). Then, the painters were the first to be afraid, and like soldiers terrified to have massacred so much around them, they began to hate their color-covered hands and they thought that the painting no longer had a source of its own and that it was exhausted (yes, except that it was them), and suddenly made so arduous and so unobvious, and so they photographed and they installed, leaving the hard and impure churning of the reluctant paste and this fault line and this wound in the color, and making the most of modern techniques that pushed everything *alongside* art, for them, and at this moment, it became the most urgent thing, to bring peace and perhaps nothing but depth around, and at least postpone as far as possible the avowal of this impossibility of painting.

But each landscape persists, all colored and monotonous and nuanced and naked and disheveled, alive finally, it is not enough to photograph them nor to calculate at the end their preparations, it will also be necessary to express why their colors make a language, which reveals what? And how do their forms, thus recovered, *correspond*? All the same, have you seen once more the immense question marks and exclamation marks which along the coasts of the world lengthen and redouble without respite? Nature, when it was born, made its own installations, more than four and a half billion years ago, the Earth was not yet, and mighty Nature then quite leisurely shaped it, perhaps by repeating itself, it alone would know from what exploded models. Launching rocks and questions onto the shores of the seas and of all the infinities. And on Earth, the colors of the land asserted themselves as lasting, that no one could have replaced, our obvious gift is to consult them. Leaving these geologies, you float on a polished aesthetic, of the pleasant and the unpleasant, with guarded limits, with non-torn, non-impure contours, where you rest, and where the tension of art is transmuted into elegance. You escape from there, and that makes another fashion, the limited-time sales of the beautiful, that we must applaud, oh people of the seasons, who are used to variations and returns. We, but which we, never figure the world as a painting nor as a representation.

Icon and retable and tragedy and comedy and tale and novella, these were specialized forms that appeared in all these specific cultures, and for example where the work of art, for being constantly accompanied by the flux of techniques and disturbances and upheavals of the human condition which resulted from them, would acquire gradually an autonomy which shaped it into one of the primary elements of this condition. A great number of peoples do not consider this possible autonomy of the work as constituting a category, rather they do not grant it. They hold the cry of the sea and the engagements of mountains and rivers and the rushing flow of clouds and the wandering of the unfaithful wind equal to the works which they create with their hands. The painting and the representation, here, there, why stop at their specificities, why question their relationship to the world? Is that giving in to a secretly instilled inclination? We can hardly guess that these creations, from the moment they started to follow their path, have gradually gathered memories of this long time where the differences between the humanities, as well as between them and their hazardous surroundings, began to grow stronger, making apparent in themselves the regret of these exiles. But these humanities then, far from considering difference as a relation and an advantage, attached themselves to it to isolate and structure and tie up, in their irremediable solitude, all conceivable specificities. Thousands of years, and of years of loneliness and withdrawal into oneself, in the gray monotony and the imperceptible variations of the light. The Earth divides into sectors and zones and portions, with shards from there and so many shadows from here. Neither convergence nor concordance. Then it happened that many works were forgotten in reserves or abandoned caves, or overexposed in the glittering mirrored galleries of the bustling societies. And others were thrown into the swamps. Differences were marked, as one would say of the sliced reliefs of a mountain under the touch of the clouds, and the works of art, in the countries which had already taken charge of the circulation of goods in the world, and which were later to assert themselves as the civilized societies, illustrated the varieties that these differences designate and isolate, the identities of living beings, of their communities and their places, *and something else as well.* And in this enormous tangle of identifications and localizations, you see, the finished works of painting and of written or spoken representations perpetuated finally the most lasting of these differences, starting from the most recent specificities of these (the molecular structures and the new energies and the rhythms of the universe and the lightning of chaos and either the mass reactions or the pleasures of publicity), pushing and lighting up counter to their former unanimity (the primordial hunger and the cold and the night and the fire and the songs to the moon and the elective force of the leaders). To remember then was to hold a gift of prophecy of the past. It was thought that the monuments, too massive, and the songs and dances, much too fleeting, and the conventions and rites, too immutable, transmitted so little. The peoples who had not subscribed to differences for the sole purpose of denying them better, who had not sunk their identities into the extreme, neither did they feel the reassuring need to draw paintings and representations that were consecrated and contrasted and distinct and soothing and so imitative of the world (it is this absence that was noted in them in deciding that they were primitive). These peoples of the sung-orality invoked the world, so it was said, rather than representing it, or else they tried to live it (but how?) instead of imitating it. At least that is what serious analysts have assumed, in trying to explain so many gaps between these cultures here and those cultures there. To give shape in any case, that is to say to create, signified in a different way, a common place too gaping for not becoming an abyss. The extraordinary diversity of the lessons of art in the world, could it be conceived of using the categories of a few models that were everywhere transposable? And why should it be so? Diversity for us is the unique and innumerable way of representing the world and rallying its people, its multiplicity is in fact the principle of its unity. From the infinite number of places in the world, humanities formerly sought, in an infinite number of ways, to rediscover the magnetic connection. And today, reading and invoking and imitating and living and representing and foretelling, and leaving and staying, meet here and everywhere else, and we have crossed the abyss, under the omens of the same scattered and convergent and multiplied arts of these same humanities, we do not yet discern by what grace this was done, nor in what ways they have gone beyond. It would certainly be the engagement of a new aesthetic, that is to say of a deeply unsettling way of conceiving a new aesthetic—that, perhaps, of *the other region of the world*, which is there, right here.

Representation, the current order of which is so ambiguous. It unfolds, it is true, you would say that it advances, but it unfolds a story, not the march of the chaos of being, which preoccupies all of us. A narrative that is thin, given this march, and which most often reflects its path as if it were that of all, of all of us. A bare story, a pure unity that is self-sufficient, pure vanity, which most often fails to enter into the totality. A story that is reinforced by a fiction, which in turn struggles to be part of the real. So, there were some fiction-makers to explain the how. They said loudly that fiction was the foundation of the art of expressing the world and they said they were the only ones to have made History, and they calmly boasted of being the first to have the right to tell stories, that is to say, once again, this narrative. The painted picture for its part had at first the task of representing, but now representation, on a page or on a stage, when it unfolded *itself*, most often closed the page or the stage. It spun around itself. Could a fiction enter *into* a part of the real? Fiction is concerned about existence, or else about its avatars, when reality henceforth jolts into the chaos of being, that is to say for us, of the inexpressible. The thing is to express the inexpressible. Where is the vanishing point? Everything is difficult. Most of these representors, this was also stupefying, did everything as most painters had done, they looked for and they found vistas at sight, so these official representors, who publicly presented themselves to you as qualified, they each dictated their closed circle back in what are reputed to be great metropolises, self-proclaimed centers of the world, used on their stages and on their pages initially graffiti, which inputs the reduction of the representation of the real, it is the limit of their ideal, to a minimal and consoling network, then derision, which leads to not being fooled by the thicknesses or obscurities of the Whole-World (and for them it is to distance themselves with full force from poetry), and then the magnification and the monumental, which seem to provide an escape from the gray and the minuscule threatening realism, as far as this appears so close to their simulacra, then the cropped language, which suits graffiti and by which they pretended to consider any language on condition that it was *ordinary* as the only matrix of what they believed to be literary language, they were not capable of any other sort of language in truth, but there they did not leave aside the so fine psychological realisms, the backbone of the novel, of those which give you the consolation of bathing in full human radiance, that is to say to spin in vertigo *above* your secretly chosen person, and they too they photographed and they installed, the arts met, a whole technical concept in extension. The photos to try to surprise time in the raw, the installations to close space to the point of death. While the photographers and installers, poor bricklayers, watched the wind go by. I have inhabited such seasons for a long time and I have witnessed these boons, escaped from the world, which strove to bypass or swallow up all the possible diversities. And why sort out such phenomena? It is because, and for all you may explode in your emptiness, you will finally admit it, they are forever part of the inextricable and inexpressible of the Whole-World, with the extremes of techniques and with what has survived the embordered places where the connivance could keep itself. We enter the Whole-World *together* (and is it already Whole-World, have we already named it so?). And the affair is lived as a promiscuity by some. Nonetheless, in the totality and in the inextricable, what is refused and takes offense, the racists and the bitter of the colonies and all these universal men and quite simply those who profit, for example, is as acute and decisive as what offers itself and reveals itself. You could not or would not want to cross out anybody. Near the landscapes however, and everywhere around, in immobile and buried places, other voices churned, in the aforesaid regions, of space and time, which did not relate to or which did not take part yet in this *new region of the world*, but which were preparing for it. Voices covered by people without voices and without writing and who had no prism to project far away their light like Isaac Newton and to decompose it like him in a rainbow. But they were learning the hard way how to read the world, it mattered not to us in which language, they sang the unique Seasons, they did not make it to the Seasons that swirled, and they depicted flowers that open at night. They did not derive any happiness from the world, on this hidden side of the Earth. Hidden from whose eyes? Do not go and make a virtue of what was misfortune. In most parts of black Africa, and today, and in many countries of the African diaspora, as much by the necessities of poverty as by a collective taste for harsh reality, the materials of the arts are found to be the closest of all to the rudiments, all fences and cements and scrap iron and forgeries and abandoned objects, thus what is elementary in the world resonates there. And this does not respond to the obsession with staged miserabilism, but to a modern and scattered and insistent and desperate attempt to establish that *magnetic connection*, which always haunts us. The order of representation is not ambiguous, but the role devolved to it becomes so, depending on latitudes and habits. Art and science have several entrances, so many exits. Every day, so close, noises bubbled in the sands, a little after noon.

Insofar as as you then interrupt the disorganized teller, you are exasperated about you don't know what, doubtless about this commotion he is making, cut him short and ask loudly, in the end what do you call the tension of art? He will not deny you reason, offering you palaver at the bottom of this poetry. And if there is a tension in any work of art, it would also be necessary to agree to recognize so many effusions, which would not be any less decisive. Let's put a question to the question. Would the effusions of art be, like those of poetry, the most important ones, through which the figures of the mind and of affect—either of knowledge and of the sharing of pleasure or of doubt and entertainment and of justice and of truth or of suffering and of closed memory and of the imperative filiation and especially of the feeling of eternity—are perhaps determined or decided? And so, do these so-called effusions of art allow us to suppose the tension in art, or to bear it? Between that which rings (the tension) and that which radiates (or which resonates, the effusion), in order to orient ourselves, we have sometimes had recourse to these notions or to these realities, which have fascinated and shaped us, sometimes even to the point of brainwashing and unreason, of existence and of being,* which we had just encountered on so remarkable, so distant traces, at the approach of the less and less sacred trees of Delphi, or on the rocks that burn from morning under the sun of Vernazza. The whole of the Mediterranean rose from its abysses, we frequented the abysses for so long. And we capsized those notions, really capsized oho! for us they have sounded and radiated (and resonated) in the roughest and most insurgent way that we could, undoubtedly for fear of going astray and thoughtless borrowings. Yet we recognized them much later, existence and being, it was then under other names, deep in the caves of hurt memory, where our stories kept watch alone.

---

* Glissant uses the terms "l'Être" and "l'étant," which I will translate as existence and being, but which may also be translated as "Being and being," as the translator of *Philosophy of Relation* has done.

Consider this thought process: being (we will mark it thus, rather than by Being, with this capital letter, which would quite needlessly ape Existence), if it is today devolved to chaos, "the chaos of being," does this mean or does it authorize us to have the presentiment that in mythical ages, in another region of space and time, of which we have never known a thing or of which we have forgotten everything it would have been considered as wandering in harmony with the idea of its own existence, and thus as very close to approaching the serenities of Existence? Once a clever genius, a universal mana, was being detached from the Divine Being? Are there serenities, or really a transcendence, of existence? Does being evolve and fluctuate, like geologies and climatic masses and the intestinal lava of planets? Can we, moreover, no more be sure of being as like a form of work clothing, perhaps even as the everyday rags, of existence, and appreciate it for what it constantly becomes, *the amount realized of all the differences of the Whole-World, and of the world, without excepting a single one?* It is also the only acceptation that we could grant to the idea of the universal. The possible quality of a universe would not escape from this totality. And what does the quantity of these differences amount to in the end? Only it, itself only, without there being any need to further suppose or to evaluate a form or a substance which *would give meaning*. If we accepted such a beautiful revolution in thought, existence would be enlightened by the immediate recognition of this realized quantity and thus would appear from then on, the absolute knowledge of that which being has there aggregated the instant intensity. This double postulation is assuredly that of poetry itself, which speaks of the order and disorder of matter and of knowledge. Existence and being, not universal, nor exclusive nor transcendent, but one to the other unanimous.

One of the strongest answers to your question, we would formulate it as one would for a postulate or an intuition: that the tension of art was an original push toward the reality (the realization) of this quantity (or totality) of differences in the world, instead of constituting, that which we wanted to maintain until our times, the search for the unknown quality *in* each of these differences, wrongly considered as an identity excepted from the others. Let us maintain this point, with regard to the cultures which have circulated, and which have rushed geographically across the world. Art would have progressed, in the unfolding of the stories of these humanities, as a push toward existence, which is, however, not an absolute of the unknown quality, but the *absolute knowledge and the recognition of this quantity (or realized totality) of the differences*, a quantity that is to come as it would be total. Art appeared at first to be thus one of the manifested variables of being, and being, by which this finite quantity of differences in the world is realized and recognized, has gradually become known, sketched then perfected as a quantity, in spite of so many forces pulling *absolutely* backwards and toward the unknown quality. But being knows no qualities, only infinite variables. In works of art, as in the real, beauty is not the splendor of truth, it is and it reveals in a work or a fact *the force of the differences which at the same time are fulfilled and already predict their relation to other differences.* Such an accomplishment comes precisely from there, from its one, its own game, it is *also this other thing* that we have been talking about. What the truly inspired in the West believed to be the absolute of unknown quality, by which they recognized beauty but by which they also preached artistic perfection, which moreover has its changing laws that no one can really hold, in truth signified the intensity of this force. Because we have the intuition of beauty each time we guess or feel in an object or an idea or a work or a passion, not simply the meeting of the same and the other (this would be a good common place), nor this so-called perfection of the forms (this would be a tautology), but the tension of a difference in itself which proposes other differences to be known and to be met. And this tension thus intervenes, in the object or in the work, between differences which can be guessed by themselves and differences *which will come to be added*, and then the tension indicates the possible of their meeting. Is beauty at the same time the reflection, the sign in the work, and the intuition, the premonition in us, of this negotiation of a difference which is confirmed by opening up to the probable, and of this attraction of a difference that will be overcome by offering itself in the same way, the negotiation turns into an attraction, it is the great circus of the world, and existence, as we have foretold and repeated, is immediately the absolute knowledge and recognition of their meeting? Yes, beauty is at this rendezvous. We have a rendezvous where the oceans, these matrices of beauty, also already meet. Spare us your storms, you boatmen of the high winds, and we love storms so much! And the beauty of beauty has taken from this, that it immediately suggests to intuition one of the dimensions of the improbable, and not from that, that it would have supposedly already ratified all truth in some evidence that to this point has been closed. The unexpected element of differences, through their mutual consecrations, is to consent to beauty this very open field of the possible. Consecrated in its turn, or diviner, beauty is forever liable not to be known or recognized, this is its grace. Prescience and consciousness and poetics of Relation were yet established there.

The first works of the humanities, engraved or painted on stone or rock, which are said to be prehistoric without one really knowing where the trace of history begins, are usually interpreted as utilitarian practices, techniques but instinctive, to better ensure the survival of a community in a hostile environment, from which we came to believe that art was first of all a way of operating, a *modus operandi*, for example for pre-figuring animals that will be hunted, in order to turn them away from the power they hold by nature and which risks destroying the community, but it is soon obvious to me, before these paintings in grottos and caves, and before all other prefiguration which was practiced under the same conditions, before what we call their beauty and which is inexplicable, before their delicacy and their lightness and this atmosphere of unreality that they have created *around them* (all humanities are capable of this finesse, and all humanities are capable of seeking the unreal in the style of a work), and that is not explained simply by the friction of time, that it is indeed an attempt to bring together the differences of the animal, for example, and those of the community that frequents it, not to really dominate the animal (even if it is seen struck across with marks and arrows and shedding its blood), but to blend into it if possible, and perhaps also for this additional purpose of warding off the threatening urgency of other differences, unknown and supported by other suddenly invading communities (and so, the figure says, *we killed it, not you*, and here is the explanation of the pickets and the lines and the blood flowing), in a way to immediately turn away the appropriations which occurred from afar, and which would not be attuned at all to the same connivances. But long before these intrusions, the paintings we are talking about illustrated the first, mad and tranquil attempt to recognize, in a way we would have termed mutual, a community and its surroundings, the adventure of an appropriation by fusion, and not by possession. Such a tension, for the first time implemented toward and between differences which would come together in opposition (those of the animal and the group, those of the place and the group), will aggregate the so inexplorable beauty of these works. Half-seen and half-guessed at in this thickness of the caves, we had the privilege of being led into those at Lascaux before they were closed, an absolute and dark pathway and which led to breathlessness, *the beauty, on the rough-hewn rocks, is this effect of a non-manifest tension and this sign of an unobvious connivance*, realized. From this beginning, art would in fact not be an exorcism, would not be a field of recipes, it would be (in each of these works which did not know themselves as works) the joint effort and this tension of differences, in so far as they all hold on to the same, and that they all connect to one another, when the same and the other were not known as separate entities. But let us see that here the other, related to oneself in a transport whose evidence is marked by fusion, was the animal, was the surroundings, represented there by chosen species, it was not these specimens of the same kind as oneself, these *similar to oneself*, natural rivals, not representable. The tension (of the differences) in these works will never have been passed directly from clan to clan (one would not figure on the darkened surfaces of the cave the silhouette of an *other* who would risk being oneself), but always, and in an independent manner for each of the clans, in and between the closest relation of these distinct family groups with only their surroundings in connivance. The relationship to this environment was tied to a total non-relationship with the various surrounding communities, human or parahuman, all ignored or fought or rejected in *their* non-existence. From then on, the irruption of such potential rivals, their wanderings which had arisen from there having unfortunately intersected with this uneasy wandering maintained here, had made it necessary for the community to renounce this act of appropriation by the fusion that had been the first artistic gesture, a divinatory act because it was accomplished by a single one but recognized as such by all, which was no longer sufficient to support the connivance with the surroundings, and made it urgent to replace it with another very realistic act of taking possession. Possession is necessary and is realized here not from the nature of the thing possessed, but according to the singular threatened presence of another possible possessor. This will be the principle of all utilitarian art. The human groups found themselves, on leaving the place, exhorted to dominate the world, those who moved around took precedence over those who *remained*, and also forgetting it but sharing it by force and blood, which they nonetheless painfully incurred so much of in order to encounter one another, and first to mortally oppose themselves to the moral rules which all disregarded difference, and which for this reason could in no way generate or balance relations. But as well, the first paintings, those of these caves and these grottos, not specific, and without ornament or board, we could not believe that they were representations of pleasure or of the proce-dures or of the instructions for use, or of the taking possession of the land and the animals born in the surrounding area. These early paintings were *magnetic connections*. The mystery is that they have come down to us when so many utilitarian works have been erased. Those who projected them in this way knew differences, not to deny them but to connect them together through these works, which thus recognized themselves as works. The renunciation of their effusion was to open the era of isolation and societal debates, Rousseau was right, and Freud too, from the point of view of what he in his turn calls civilization, and of course the advent of art that has been called realistic will begin there, and with a veritable taking of possession. The representation of totems will connect this realistic art to the symbolist style of identitarian figurations. The fundamental solitude of the clan had thus been succeeded by the wars of the tribes and then the isolation of the communities. We do not recognize under what conditions the human groups had appeared, from or alongside which primate cousins, and we discover only on a fairly precise occasion the range of the iconic representation of handprints, these first signs at the same time of difference and identity and action, but also of meetings and concert, their clear outlines edged with aura and shadows, which accompanied or replaced on the rough walls of some of these caves that of the animals and the surroundings, perhaps indicating for such new artists a detour and a return to oneself and to one's gesture and to one's act, a call perhaps to the literal nature of the world. But it is also true that subsequently, in the histories of the human groups, the unclassifiable search for beauty will have been carried out essentially along these two paths, in all incommunicable and which will sometimes uncross, and that is until today, the ancient quest for the first appropriation and its transport of connivance, a secret investigation, unsure of itself, and yet very imperious in the trembling of its obscurities, which reveals in works and objects the tension, to the places where differences meet and where this beauty will therefore be distinguished, and on the other hand and on a completely different side, the accumulation and the very public application and the exploitation of these systems of techniques, that is to say of these new rules agreed and applied in common, and which sometimes will have led to how much unanimity, and in particular on the estimation of and the taste for the beautiful. And we will perhaps no longer have to choose, this time dealing with always variable beauty and no longer just of the beautiful (which often assimilates to fixed beauty), between the vertigo incurred in secret by a few and the unanimity decided by the most. In the early ages in any case, which we will hesitate to call prehistoric, of the species, or else, from the prefigures of those stories which gradually distinguished the various humanities among themselves, the work of art appeared long before the troubled workings of war, and aesthetic presence and activity long preceded ethical rest.

One will characterize by the name of civilization the long temporal periods *during* which, in the West mainly, but also, before and after this appearance, in the Middle East and in Egypt, in China, in Russia, and in Mongolia, and in Japan, and in the continents which were not yet the Americas, the humanities thus learned to know one another through incessant confrontations, dramatic upheavals, which little by little assembled the communities into established identity units, moreover, making them increasingly piled up on themselves, and made them totally and unanimously opposed to one another. The natures of their modes of government and their real controls would provide the essential elements of their internal wars, economic domination will lead to external conflicts, but it is the splendors of their arts which attest to their duration. From which it emerges from the histories of these civilizations that art was amply considered by them as an indefatigable enterprise of improvement of all techniques, of invention and improvement of means and modes of expression, and it resulted that the history of this art, that is to say of these illustrated techniques, almost ended up becoming the principle occasion of artistic emotion, and that the works have most often contributed for example to perfecting the possibilities of expression of the instruments as well as their mastery, then the notion of performance begins to generalize, and the rules finally above all intended to facilitate their own and well-polished adaptation to new intentions or obligations. The harmony of the fellow human reigned over sensibilities, the works of art move away from the revelation of the differences, ignore the impact of the conflicts and the overriding of these differences, they become the declared ornaments of the new identities of the peoples-states and their closed places, and the ceremonial clothing of their expansions and their exactions in the world. This is what was said, exporting civilization. Two constants marked these periods. Artists, first of all, for the pleasure of complying with the rules, have never really given up on the secret ambition of renewing with the energies of the world, and of reconsidering and daring the old original attempt at knowledge by fusion and connivance. This is what immediately convinces us in a poem by Rutebeuf or one by Villon, or in some very benign sonnet by Ronsard. I speak thus of these encounters where civilization is reputed to have flourished without restraint or remorse, where there extended a double scope of art, namely the said ornament (or the said technique, which professes the rules of unanimity), and the obscure, which keeps difference alive. And beauty then gave its tension away under its charms. And so, the pure-impure and hard civilizational glow, but also the call of the profound and the negotiation-attraction of these differences. We will perhaps spot, throughout the histories of these humanities, who then singularized themselves in nations, and accompanying this silent sedition of artists, more or less secret organizational movements, which strike us by their harsh insistence and permanence, and even in the almost unknown places where these stories of glory are located, and most of these organizations strive to morbidly strengthen the bonds of single root identity, or on the contrary to stretch them in a revolution or a revelation no less absolute, they are unperceived avatars of the identical, of which here are some of those that we have been able to identify historically, initiatory brotherhoods in Greece and Rome and all the delirious and ephemeral religions and the heresies of the first Christians and the Cathars and the Félibres and the Round Tables and Raymond Lulle and so many other mystics and the pure alchemists and the libertines and the mystery of the first banks born from usury and the East and West India Companies and the Jewish and Arab mystics and already the Hashishins and the more or less initiatory religious orders and the Temple and the dashing Rosicrucians and the Freemasons and the more sober companions and the innumerable secret and political societies and the racial domination fanatics and the odious and the ridiculous and the heroes of all stripes, from the Carbonari to the ancestors of the Ku Klux Klan, and the initiates of everything and nothing of almost all the countries of the south of this North and the swarming religious sects of the continents and the archipelagos and all these initiatory families, either Chinese or Japanese or Brazilian and the mafias of the two hemispheres, of which it does not seem that the sole requirements of security justify or fully explain the so complex rules of operation nor the strict ceremonial of secrecy, and then finally the very powerful economic and financial consistories (where inseparable profit and identity are both invisible), of which we will never know where the meetings are being held, and it seems that there, in these events so widespread over the world, a double story is hatched, civilizations and their tormented reverse, a story that has not yet met up with itself, and which has not yet joined what happened in Africa or in the isolated Oceanies, centers of strictly endogenous cultures, except that they have provided so much in deportations and contributed to diasporas, and in so many other solitudes of the world. A double history, and the debate over the differences which come to the surface of the conscience, torment and knot the unconscious, known or consented or rejected, with the lots of intolerances and the piles of crimes and the heaps of absurd sacrifices and blind ramblings, which the Apollonian masses of golden rules will have accompanied by representations and the rigid principles of beauty and the decrees of good speech. In European history, the acute subversion of the baroque intervened to bar these categories but they had to be exported thereafter to the good and welcoming lands of South America, where they flourished and went somewhat crazy. Another constant in the slow development of these cultures and civilizations has been no less firm and remarkable, and it is the habit that was adopted, so serene and generalized, of sharing the most officially in the world the world itself, in learned councils and in big papal bulls and drafts and very commercial agreements and peace granted or torn off and cynical arbitrations and do Africans have a soul and yes no maybe and well they have one and the borders drawn with a line on loose and random maps of the world and anticipated dispatches from unknown and almost inaccessible countries and memories uprooted without recourse and in the end inverted justifications and even today official international organizations of all kinds, who fill the stage, and the G6, G7, G8, who each year feel the pulse of the world and misjudge the measures to conserve the systems in place. At the same time when the safeguarding is assured once and for all, and fortunately, of the *Mona Lisa* and the other so-called treasures of the heritage of humankind. And: treasures are valuable from the moment where they are deported to the Centers. This bailiwick of property was hardly discreet, and propriety was reduced to a minimum. But the crossings for millennia have nonetheless been established and sustained between so many regions that were so little known to one another. The ravages, they are a common place, sometimes generate their remedies. Even if the concrete memory of these contacts is mixed with reluctance and reformed visions and an equal resentment on both sides of these ancient clashes. Be that as it may. Feeling astonished at the sumptuous work dictated on the return from his travels by the Venetian Marco Polo, he was then held in jail because no one wanted to accept the wonders he was telling, *Conversing the World*, I sometimes worried if it was a question of conversing, of showing by imagining, or of converting, and the division of the world, that is to say of sharing the thing crudely. This was not a maneuver allotted to the West alone, yet it has operated a lot in this way.

We all needed to know the Greek pre-Socratics and the Taoists of Asia, and to approach the principles of the sacred books of Egypt or India or the Ante-Americas, books of the dead or books of memory, and not only to drift in these cultures, but also to experience what being was and what could not have been there, and the recognition of existence, and if their sharing in these books was abundant, their legitimate presence. Meditate on why or how the intuition of existence and being arose and expressed itself from the same Mediterranean place where appeared the three most important monotheistic religions in the histories of the humanities, and from which arose subsequently the all too famous general scope of sciences and those techniques, and also the conquerors and the discoverers. Metaphysics and enterprise. Conquests of knowledge and harsh subjugation of all strangers. Was this really a predestination, or the logic of parallel thought processes? Were they right, those who observed, following the example of Prospero the wise, that to control rational, and cabalistic knowledge, was to control the debate of the world? Since then, we have all needed to hear in real life the storytellers of the Whole-World, which was only *what the world lacked in order to be the world*, and Caliban's complaint. With them the differences add up, being is perfected. Their tales are not recitals, which is why they are stories of the world. (Are you saying that being is a pure and simple quantity? Yes, a quantity, but neither pure nor simple!) You distinguish the question of why from that of how, but it is the same if it so happens, and existence is inseparable from being. And thus do we conceive that the works of art, however various may be the infinity of their detail in the infinite number of possible situations, either that it has worked its trace in the most extreme technicalities, and whether it has lasted as close as possible to these thicknesses of the worlds, have indeed remained at the height of the realization (of the totality) of the quantities of differences, even though these works would have seemed to move away from them. And for everyone there is a discreet course of the appearance of works and of the estimation of the situation of the world, along which art does not arrange its works as in a series of unilaterals, because what we call being is their exploded field of resolution, and existence their true denial at the same time as their recognition. From which we will have to designate to existence and being other names and new meanings. They may have borrowed from hidden or secret personalities, in uncrowded parts of the world, that is, in places where the inhabitants would have first considered every elsewhere as a non-place. Or they would be species of zombies that endlessly roam spaces, at least we would like to interpellate them in this form. Or else Spirits, for example, would be the energetic existence and the material being, an energetic spirit and a material spirit, just as it has been said that there are animal spirits. The lesson of these accumulations and these alchemies, very visible in the histories of these humanities, is that beauty is the secret receptacle of all differences, and that it announces them to whoever wants to know. It devotes to them the tension which in any work, or in any given of the world, elected by us, manifests it. He who thus has conceived the work of differences will immediately conceive of the works of art, or at least part of their uncertain finalities. But we will soon come to other conclusions, less systematic perhaps.

You meditate on what you know about the creations of Asia, where the sun rises. Put yourself in Asia, you might say that the sun rises in the West, which for you will of course be in the East. This is why men have seen so long that this Sun revolves around the Earth, because the fixed certainties are in the North and in the South, and East and West are human variables, East and West, because of this, have lost their geophysical intensity. Let us observe a generalized magnetization of the movements of the humanities, the conquests and the invasions carried from the North to the South (the invasions pushed toward the North, Carthaginians or Arabs, seemed in the long run to be malfunctioning), the emigrations from the South to the North. The old East–West relationship is bifurcated, immigration and invasion run in both directions, even if we then observe that the West (Alexander then Islam to the east, Columbus and the Christians to the west, colonizations everywhere and for a long time in the world, the Nazis in all directions too, but without any lasting hold) moved around much more than the Orient. I say the Orient because I'm very intrigued by the imperative balance of the Occident, which one can say has designated itself thus, therefore I feel authorized to take together China and India and Japan and the Indonesias and the Polynesias, rejecting from this group the countries that I would not like, like a good exoticist who chooses his stop-off points. Not being able to put in disorder the infinite differences which arise there, it becomes more or less obvious to me that what was common to these cultures will not have been different ways of living and of relating their differences (that would be a kind of common ground), but a generalized custom, to impose on all differences, starting with oneself or the other, an absolute and spectacular restraint, and to consider the works of art and those of Nature first as a framework, temporal rather than spatial, or rather where time has become a space, very conducive to the rigorous elevation of these differences. The ceremony is therefore the first measure of what moves excessively and becomes confused, or of what stagnates too much. So, *the cry is a neurosis, fertile and cadenced with silence.* And the hard hierarchies and the *weighty* clothes and the exasperated politeness and the ritual make wild and ice-cold entries on this stage where the aforementioned differences were played out, whose attractions–repulsions seem to us from then on overdetermined. The ritualization of differences limits their expansion, hence it is that art and its works would not have here (there) the purpose of illustrating or revealing, as we would have expected in spite of everything, the mutual impact of these differences, but quite on the contrary their purpose was to differ with very elaborate minutiae the revelation of this impact. A practice not of time that is exhausted but of time that is suspended. Beauty is not there the sign of tension or the announcement of connivance, it is the most knowing (and therefore the slowest) possible accompaniment of this difference. By the most transparent and the most elaborate and the most refined of techniques, but finally the most inextricable, to contain or disconcert as far as desirable the most obscure parts of knowledge and of its desire. The art of maintaining as high as possible an order and a balance at any risk, has taken over from the art of predicting from the works or the facts of the real the secret place where beauty is formed, but it is always the differences which are the object of these cold about-turns. And thus, we suppose that the Occidental arts underline and raise the differences to guard against them, the same place where the arts of the Orient envelop them with a time of restraint and thus organize the differing. Can we say that? It is true, we admit, that we experience these ways of *feeling ideas* every time we dare not orient ourselves to the full of this matter, just as little known to us. Let us therefore use an unexpected word which is quite appropriate: that the appearance of such general conceptions often makes up for, and by the grace of intuition, a real ignorance.

When the differences of the world, in the world, meet, the varieties, which they recognize, multiply just the same. It is because the differences, by adding and changing, little by little situate being, and that we feel it as the only remnant of that which always moves and changes. The difference is at the lively beginning of the movement, and not the identical, or identity. The harmony of the similar is neutral and fruitless, but the meeting of differences, and which is not the harmony of opposites, is accomplished in and by a mutual going beyond which is the basis of the unexpected of the Whole-World. This hard work of differences is neither harmonious nor reasonable. The accumulated varieties, the whole of which shapes diversity, go through diversions which change their natures as well as through proliferations which bring them together by opposing them, unpredictable operations. Diversity is thus the motor-matrix of the chaos-world. Let us examine this accumulation as fleetingly as possible. That the varieties, given in the intuition of the impacts of the differences and not in the perpetuity of what would have been a nature or an essence, outline the modalities of existence or of relation of a people or of a community or of all landscapes, or of an energy of the world. And that finally diversity, this proliferation of varieties, founds Relation. That Relation weaves its relationships not only, if it occurs, between two or more of these varieties (or identities), but more generally between everything and everything, and in the unpredictable. That while we say that differences locate being in space and time, we whereby reiterate, not that being is limited in space and time, but that they twist it into Relation. That in this way, and in the same way, we cannot distinguish between the varieties of mankind and the identities of their surroundings. That identities are varieties that discover themselves, yet that these discoveries are not limited to the field or the sole *role* of consciousness. That we experience the throbbing but ignored temptation, moreover never really put into action—art is no mimicry—to always start again the primordial gesture of the connivance, formerly accomplished with the first paintings, those of the grottos and the caves from before what we call history. And that, by this inclination of an unrecognized desire, and perhaps instinctively rejected, art presents itself more readily to us as universal and immaterial, in the form of an absolute reality, set outside of history. That we want by this to repeat this gesture, but that we always hesitate to undertake it. That the histories of art in the so-called civilizations are then, and by us, although we do not participate in them, felt as disengaged from the histories of the humanities, wholly apart, a kind of completely transcendental path which would be made of a series of sparkling adornments offered as an absolute gift and without a cause, and from which we would not dare distance ourselves. Such a dazzling non-historicity has long been the guarantor of the sublime elevation of art. We must, after such an accumulation, then try to summarize (to measure) these processes, with statements that are so monotonous and so affected. But the world that they manifest is not.

Thus were accumulated the modes of identity of these creatures of art, fashioned by the walking and trading human groups, so many works aroused from their imagination and their practice, to which we must return, and which enter into the play of Relation at the same time and in the same way as the varieties of the peoples and the lessons of the unknown peoples and the colors of the landscapes and the ways of Nature. Their unpredictable diversions meet, it is one of the secret articulations of the chaos-world. Inspired, and deduced from hard work, these works of art and knowledge often seek to rediscover the gift of complicity in the totality, of which we have recognized the trace, and more often still to consecrate an unanimity of techniques. Thus, we can admit, without constraining ourselves to idealism, that they inform the real and compose it. We consider then that art and knowledge are not unilinear, that their modes of intervention in the real are wholly contradictory and infinite and scattered and concentrated and that they do not concern the real and that they occupy it entirely. And again, as regards the meeting of differences, that each variety or each identity, in this space-time which gave birth to the stories of the humanities, comes to change in itself by exchanging with others, but without getting lost, nor losing its nature, and these no more so, which exchange and change in themselves and with others. That Relation is neither diffusion nor confusion. We realize that works of art are the implicit and real relays of such a movement, and for example the *Stèles* from the edge of this path that Victor Segalen traveled in China. Finally, it becomes very conceivable to us, and even if it is not a hard science, that the notions of existence and being, at one time in the histories of the humanities, were established and divined and imagined unceasingly to accompany this resistible movement toward a realized quantity of the differences of the world: being in order to deploy its machinery and its domain and the field, and existence in order to disembody both the knowledge and the recognition, and also the resistance that was necessary, that it was always necessary to oppose, to appose to the movement, in order precisely that it was completely organic, that is to say that it results from differentials which attract and accord, and not mechanically, a skein of similar entities without returns. The beingness of existence has always been absolutely to resist that which is *animated* by mechanicity alone. And today we discover that Relation is not (at all) a coarse, bare, raw, and blunt relationship, but *also* the exercise of an alchemical complexity, the elements of which it will be necessary for us to disentangle clearly, in and around us. (Do you mean that existence would be like a person, perhaps a divinity, in any case much more than an entity? No, no which is absolutely not. But if existence is also interdependent with being, it is revealed by the same fact that it would be the spirit and the energy of the diverse!) What the human groups, who considered this notion so necessary, called then existence was the energy of the world in motion, for us today it is the meeting of differences, or at least their absolute recognition, and the foreknowledge that we hold of them. And the energy of the world in motion displaces the differences and organizes their inexpressible elements. In such connections, and to add to the mystery of existence, art appeals to us here and not as a pure and immaterial and eternal force, as we shared yesterday the great beliefs and the common idea, but concrete and dense and unbreakable, and all the more successful that it has engaged with the things and matters of land and sea, sources and providences of all the others, and that it has limited itself to them. However, works of art no longer attempt to transmit or carry traces or magnetic connections, but above all they become effective bearings in and for the examination of reality. Not utilitarian, but *entered into the real*. It seems to us, and contrary to everything we felt before, that these works of art actively partake of restive being, and that they renounce now the so-refined evidence of existence. As if, at times, they decided to conquer their autonomy at once and then chose to defend the threatened cause of humans. But did they have to give up their ambition to find the trace and the magnetic connections? We no longer decide perhaps between the injunctions formerly made to all art, to have to support a universal and to confirm a reality, or else not to wander in illegible propitious things. This sparse formulation is sufficient for me for the moment, as strange as it is obscure.

Languages spoken and then written, just as much as works of art, have been the lasting and changing tracks of the advance of this movement of quantifications (let us estimate thanks to them how the gap between the colors of the world grew and our reflexes of ideas and words), and sung or oral languages, are the first instruments of exploration, hazardous and fruitful, of this quantification. Beauty deposits its tension in all languages, equal, unpredictable. In both, *langages* appear. The dead languages and the languages of secrecy (to be deciphered) make up reserves, a material of the unconscious, between the languages which are spoken then written and the languages sung, or spoken, on the one hand, and on the other hand the *langages*, which are there structured then related. Far from the tracks of languages, at the very depths of the bushes of words, these reserves are dedicated to the linguistic survival of all, they remind us that even when they have disappeared, languages have left traces in us, and that perhaps already stir in us languages *that will come*, which are our differences of the future. Spoken-written languages are thus, and also, not only lasting tracks, but traces, which tend to base on the trembling absolute of existence, whereas *the cry is a visitation*, from which comes sometimes the reputation which they claim loudly to have been dictated by a god, spoken-sung languages are actively operative and on the contrary strive to hold and cross cleanly over the hard jolts (or chaos) of being. The *langages* created in the modern spoken-written languages relate these differences. Languages establish and *langages* locate. But the current creolizations of languages and cultures, of mores and customs and the brutal mutations arising from conflicts and massacres and the so slow adaptations secreted by the pleasure of secret frequentations, soon lead to and discover new offerings, for example of idioms, both living languages and critical *langages*, which themselves engage the revision of the One, that is to say also of existence, which is an absolute recognition of it, just as it is of the movement of the differences of the world, and these same idioms also undertake the examination of any surrounding language, whenever it is deemed to trace or follow an absolute approach to existence. So are made Creole idioms, at once languages and *langages*. Any *langage* whose specificity is first stated as literary and artistic formulates and proffers an organic critique (and a reform) of the languages in which it has worked. The language sometimes fades away, but the *langage*, which carries a work, persists and endures. Unless we consider one of those languages whose work, inscribed in fragile orality, may have perished and disappeared entirely, or has withdrawn to the bottom of these reserves of the unconscious over which we have no control. And it is necessary to believe that the spoken-sung languages continue to make traces in us, watchtowers that we will meet one day. However, these languages take each time the radical detour of the established rhetorics, they fulfill, *outside any context of art or literature, a literary and artistic function*, of questioning the means of representation, as did the *langages* forged in the spoken-written languages, and these sung-spoken languages happily practice accumulation and repetition and assonance and circularity which combines with repetition to sketch spirality, all operations so uneconomical from the point of view of the use of speech and writing, and these languages are thus both by themselves, and immediately after their appearance, critical *langages*. Each *langage* thus created strives to bring us closer not to the economical perfection of speaking, but to the achievable quantity of differences, which ignores the concern for any perfection whatsoever but stems from tensions or reveals to itself this beauty, of which existence will immediately affirm the absolute recognition. And in its turn this *langage* will consider existence as the guarantor of such a realized quantity, but this same language will falter at the same time and with the same energy, this is its paradoxical advantage, against the temptations of the absolute posted in the language or languages it will have frequented, even if it is nevertheless existence that would best signify these temptations of the absolute. The languages-*langages* of sung orality are much more vigilant, on these points, than the spoken-written languages or even the critical *langages* resulting from these written languages, because they (these languages-*langages*) have had the experience of entanglements and the inextricable. They adapt themselves, and even if in a dizzyingly brief fashion, to fractal realities and to the ruptures of the world. In this, they teach us that *writing* knots itself at the same time as it exposes its object, that this knot becomes this object, we would say *there is no writing innocently*, and that what we say and speak is *everything* in the form of what we write. Each *timoune* (Have we seen what *a timoune* is? Did we recognize it?) is a child in this world, *timoun dan moun*, not already by this symbolism of its age or by the reality of its wandering, these two situations full of the sense of brevity, but because it pronounces non-absolute languages, which it perhaps led *into* the imperious language that has been proposed to or imposed on it but from which it escapes infinitely, we do not know not if it speaks or writes them, it is all the same, it usurps the most advanced techniques to do this, and because it also stumbles toward unheard-of *langages* that it shapes instinctively. *Langages* which suggest and critique the absolutes and the excesses of belonging. Thus, the *briefest* communities (the fractal solidarities of streets, and the age groups in isolated groupings, as well as the speakers of the same agreed or fabricated *langage*, or the members of equally hazardous gatherings, astonished to find one another there just as *multiple*) are perhaps the most decisive for us, or at least they seem to us the most favorable to a revealing initiation into the world of agreed differences. Then we become naively the *timounes* of the *new region of this world* toward which we stumble, and that we intuit, in and around us.

Of space, this *new region of the world* is a totality, the first to be truly realized in the history of humankind. A diffracted non-totalitarian totality, the conjunction of differences tends to leave none of them *aside*. We enjoy *geographizing* this increasingly accomplished realization of the quantities of differences in the world. We no longer describe the landscapes, we talk about them and pant for them, like when we intrude into these caves. We put them in relation, here and here, and this is the real field of human imaginaries. High and low points are the real signals of the meetings of the differences between them and of their agitations within us. Even so, we do not yet reconcile small and large deserts, lagoons and lakes, hills and pitons. It is that we always hold fast to our closed places. We admit that a difference is not an alienation, nor the valid reason for an apartheid, that it is in all, the organic element of a Relation. We were born from this movement, even though at the first gesture we rejected it, and we reject it for this ancient reason that we have always, since the first taking possession, tracked our places like so many stiff, reductive semblances. But voilà, our places are now open, and time has reopened, a multiplicity of spaces radiating in the organicity of infinite geographies, that are never unique, of course distinctly cut out under the lights of any moon, yet so passionately mixed across the varieties of their range. Astonished, we finally receive the lesson of Gaston Bachelard's work, and we conceive that the colors of the landscapes (because we hesitate to consider the structures, whose inextricable multiplicity still intimidates us), these colors that we relate to the being of the world, are in solidarity with our most secret reactions, be they elementary or elaborate. Thus, we believe with the poets that it is given to us to restate the complicity of things. However, we used to calculate, as I did at the tormented beginning of this book, the gaps that rushed in between them and us, between our desires and the expanse of the seas, and between our incomprehensible words and the clarity of the sea, and between our exultations and the depth of the forests, so we brooded over tales burdened with idealisms and materialisms, and we solicited with great balance of conviction the flat and the useful and the concrete and compassion and beneficence. Thus, we tried to forget the first gesture of art, the magnetic effusion, the attempt to merge with the energies of the world, but there, and always, we are haunted by it. The original artistic event left in us this trace which cannot disappear and which also could not be displayed accurately. So that, in an elusive way, art is irreplaceable in us but is in us allusive and problematic. So, we agree to these dreams that are also themselves concrete, which already carried us toward the limits, Mars and the worlds which one calls external, the clearest way to leave the torment of the right-here. Isn't this adventure in space a quest, perhaps the last, for the *magnetic trace?* Could the universe be the cave in which we grope around to find the unsuspected wall and to detect there this connection, this trace, or to mark it there? Until the dizziness of the difference sticks a third eye between your eyes, and you enter that region, at once of here and of there.

Of time, this new region is therefore a diversity, the first which allows us to such an extent to juxtapose or commute systems of duration that we consider cultural, or historical, the duration of our collectivities, and not the duration of our particular existences, and that we considered previously to succeed one another rigidly along an imperative line, or else to organize themselves into alienated hierarchies, and now we hurtle over them in all directions and we become their intimate and tormented travelers. And the first of the diversities of time which allows us to transform into moving networks these time periods in which we had become stuck. Now our spaces flee and move away infinitely and they seem to escape us. But, have we really inhabited them? Our times in turn become spaces, which project in starry configurations. The future is made of stars. So when we think and recognize that this is alive *for all of us,* whether we be gaunt bearers or haughty carriers of memories, and street haranguers or silent stifled passers-by, and technicians of so many spectacles of the world or gaping naked audiences lying in front of their screens and designers of liberated bodies or women frozen under the snow gripping their children who suck their stone-like breasts, and troubled sons of commanders or resolute sons of fieldworkers, and those who have drunk by the moon or those who wither on their feet, and those who tremble to the thousandth of a millimeter for the arrival of their rockets or those who see rockets falling in the distance without knowing why, for all these we signal a tacit consent to such new commutative ensembles and to this realized totality of places and to this gathered diversity of the ages, which ceaselessly make the *other region of the world* into which we have entered, right here. But it is never true that we are naive in this region, it is not a refuge of dreams nor a fantasy of hope. Also, we no longer stumble into it. It is not a chosen land. It does not belong to anyone. *As you already know, without knowing anything yet*, we shout it out and call it Whole-World.

SPINNING REALITIES AND OVER-DETERMINED FANTASIES, AND PIECES OF DIFFERENCES AND SUBLIME GEOGRAPHIES AND THE ONLY UNSHARED POVERTY.

Oh suffering, like winter at the sources of the depths … While we wander far from the misfortunes of the peoples of the world, and we believe ourselves to be preserved from them by this distancing, but we do not yet feel ourselves distracted from them through too much indifference, we have an intuition of what the sum of these misfortunes could be. As if to imagine the totality of it would reduce the weight of each particular suffering. So, the torments of humanity have no end? Aesthetics, which is not an ethic and which does not presuppose a moral, however allows one to appreciate this end. We vilify the scandalous beliefs according to which the apocalypses presage a renewal of the youth of the world, an idea which is in no way more acceptable than the old fantasy of catastrophic annunciations of the end times. But at least, in this very excess of the current deperditions, the common generalized place sketches the theory that it is the end of an era, this quaternary era, water and ice and the seas and the heat and the mountains and the cold and the clouds and the coasts and the species, change, and that beyond the eternities of so many deadly upheavals, humankind will inhabit a new geological cycle: our species is four ages old, even if it appeared at the very extreme end of the fourth, and it will go right from this quartidi to a quintidi, it will be fifth, a fifth age, in short it will enter into this fifth era, kingdoms of snow or cultures drowned in the deserts or a *submarine* universe or maybe urbanism of the bush or republics of lost islands or not much, the flat, the uniform, the machine, we know nothing of them, it will simply be necessary, if possible, to survive the cataclysms that will accompany by necessity the aging or the mutation or the passage. And it is a kind of logic without nuance which runs through these estimates and which authorizes the linking together of the seismic and geological upheavals of this planet and the too brutal action of the humanities (all violence is bad violence), whether they devastate geographies at their mercy or that through it we massacre entire peoples, as in the good old days of great invasions and grand colonizations. The movement is the same and the effect is the same and the furies and injustices of these humanities add to the furies and fatalities of Nature, and the advantage of it is that we quite willingly abandon the intention or even the weary habit of opposing them, in the tetanic stupefaction into which we are thrown by their excesses ... *Oh suffering, this beating of the wind in the streets* ... The oppressors no longer need to be striving to reduce the oppressed, it suffices to maintain them in their precarious conditions of existence, Nature then does the rest. It is necessary only not to be too careful with this Nature and rather jostle with it bravely, in the name of the holy laws of profit for example. All of this is just commonplace. The theories or ideologies of liberation, which have grown since the Western eighteenth century, heritages of the well-known complicity between the idea of existence and the ideas of the sciences, and which, moreover, have aged themselves, for never having known how to sense the inextricable elements of the Whole-World, thus disappear before the false prophecies of the too real planetary danger, which is of the order of the trial by ordeal, and split in the noise of appeals for compassion, which obliterate willpower and often disguise new surreptitious forms of submission.

The assured aging, from the fourth to the fifth age, is the very thing that we suggested would foreshadow a renewed youth of the world, with its most recent convoys and loads and vomit of weary terrors. But fortunately, perhaps, the *timounes* will no longer accept it. We do not call so and solely, *timounes*, the children born of the archipelagos, as in certain parts of the Caribbean where a *timoune* is a young person, a child indeed (and therefore *an moune*, a grown-up person, an adult). No, we will not confine ourselves to this fashion that newspapers around the world have called a vogue for youth, which entrusts to the youth and to them only, by a sort of heavy genealogical right, any mission of renewal of the sermons and practices of peoples. We will however retain the idea, and we will come to the uncertain etymology of the Creole word *moune*, or *moun*, from the English *man*, or from the French *monde*, or from somewhere else altogether, and we will consider that *a timoune* is a new full will or full intuition before the new reality of the Whole-World. Thus a very old bushman, where the bush pathetically persists, is perhaps a *timoune*, and a child abandoned on the streets of Metropolis is perhaps a *timoune*, and an august or sovereign assembly, supported by all the qualities of the most successful technologies, is perhaps a reunion of the lives *vié mouns*, older or elderly persons, who do not understand what we have called globalism, which intends to oppose the mechanical effects of globalizations, and will designate the realities and the intuition of a realized number of differences in the world. And everything is obscure in everything, including the harshness of the *timounes* not to take the pretext of this passage from one era to another, from this real quaternary to this supposed quinary period, a moreover compulsory going beyond if it is in terms of millennia that we are thinking, to indulge in the fatalities of predicted and apocalyptic histories. We are all young in the Whole-World, there are no old and wise civilizations, nor recent and savage ones, and to consider a very old culture, and from the unique point of view of a genealogical line consecrated by the West, as incapable of entering fully into globalism, precisely because of its ancient nature, it would allegedly be too worn or too disillusioned or disenchanted with everything, this is to admit that its movement has not led like that of other cultures to prepare new varieties of peoples' identities, and that could not be. The quantities of differences in the world are not subtracted from difference, there are no useless people, even if uselessness could have been considered as a freedom or a privilege, the *vié mouns* are the people of the world who simply do not want to experience the world as it travels and changes, and are afraid of it. Bombings and famines and massacres and pathogenic miseries and waves and furies, and yet the peoples are gathering on the new shoreline. It is only that we do not distinguish the limit of the lands and the seas, nor that of the waters that come from the land and of the salty waters. But we meditate on this dimension, globalism, which we have suggested to be recognized as such, during the debates and discussions which have generally focused on globalizations, at the turn and at the beginning of the 2000s. It was really a collective feeling, there were many who, with one voice that was different each time, spoke in the same way and then adopted the idea that dehumanized mechanisms and the cold denials of globalizations are to be fought first by the dynamic organicities of globalism. Globalizations are inevitable, they bring good and bad, and for this globalism is all the more invaluable to us. This is not a refrain, we all tremble from this tremor. We plan the *changing of the ages* in order to reassure us!

In the private districts of the big and small cities of these opulent worlds, the immigrant communities either ignore or clash with one another, having come from the desolated regions of the Earth, and their differences are all the more apparent and irremediable that they oppose one another on a very uncertain terrain, that of the dominant host community. They first experienced the sea, the deserts, the frozen borders, the fences, that are sometimes even electrified, the checkpoints, they have left their skins and their bones on the barbed wire, in the hot waters where drift by necessity the boat people, now they are endeavoring, if that is the right word, to earn three pounds or five euros a day, the rich countries have practiced trafficking of these people and will push them back when they no longer need them, and why these mephitic paintings, in other isolated and muddy or dusty countrysides, in the distance, abandoned groups search for a little water, in the alleys of the shantytowns ten-year-old children kill as on an assembly line, and why these paintings of sulfur and rot? *It is because the eternal spinning movements of the evolutions of the peoples and the changes, accommodations and reversals of their imaginations did not hurtle across our histories at the same lively pace as the acknowledged or secret conjunctions of these peoples, and thus we find that the quantities of differences accumulated throughout the world have begun to be perfected and to be recognized as such, when the communities which support these differences have not yet realized to regard any given difference as an advantage and not as an occasion to show contempt.* Thus, do the countries receiving immigrants imagine absorption policies, and France for example, which has the formidable knack of assimilation, which is perhaps a form of generosity, and whose proponents will not doubt that a normal person, and well enough advised, would not hesitate to declare themselves French, has decided on a policy of integration, chosen or forced, which implies for each immigrant, when they find themselves immersed in unfavorable conditions, a de facto renunciation of their original culture, alongside the suffocating conditions of their new closed places of residence, and which sometimes becomes a culture of withdrawal and resentment. The United Kingdom, on the other hand, whose governments, perhaps out of respect for the other, could not really consider a Bantu national as a full-time and long-term British citizen, pursues a policy based on the idea of community, which also risks isolating the immigrant, and to the extent that their living conditions remain precarious, in the very distance from their original culture, which becomes a kind of automatic culture. The other countries, for example Germany and the Netherlands and the United States (the latter too large and too powerful for problems to arise there under such threatening conditions), improvise, from one to the other of these exclusive choices. These large immigration patterns have repercussions on the destinations and flows of small local or regional immigrations. Not a single program envisages a true *politics of Relation*, the open recognition of differences, without these being brought as a whole at the expense of a determining communitarianism (there is not a single communitarian declaration which is addressed to the French populations settled in Ivory Coast or in Kourou in Guyana, they don't need one) as well as the open and stabilized practice of attractions and oppositions between these differences, without the attraction leading suddenly to dilutions, or opposition to antagonisms. This would be to live the beauty of the world. We know that the levers of these businesses are for the exclusive ends of profit, that there are other kinds of savage immigration, in countries which are truly unprotected and which could not lead anyone back to their borders nor control these new flows, and these are the invasions of all-powerful money, the influx of technicians, and the irremediable investments in these countries of the South, for revenues which will immediately go elsewhere. The loop becomes infernal on sight, most of the receiving countries may have reached a critical saturation point, and at the beginnings of the chain the poverty of the countries providing immigrants continues to grow. But, on another level, and on the same occasions, the reversal of imaginaries is even slower and more difficult, the humanities have lived so much in the closure of their places and in the vows to close their identities, there where from now encounters and concordances multiply, that it has become very difficult to simply want to go beyond these fixed frameworks. Peoples have mixed together for so long, and are still slaughtering one another. Spiritualities are transformed unthinkingly into so many peaceful and deadly forms of intransigence, a domestic, quotidian fascism, or into spectacles of delirious refusal. New beliefs are taken to an insane degree of absurdity, which everyone considers and accepts. And in the most well-equipped and technical societies, *Capitalism is Freedom*, it is clear and proclaimed and claimed and placarded at road junctions, and money and freedom go together, privileged castes are no longer strictly hereditary, and destitute peoples and wandering individuals are every time sent back to their fate. Then the idea is reinforced that nobody is responsible anymore and that everyone, each individual, will get out of this maelstrom, if they really think about it. The accomplished autonomy of the human person, one of the commonplaces of democracy, is mired in the organized anarchy of incompatible individual interests. Everyone is distracted by saving, all alone, a humanity, albeit virtual. In poor societies, however, pandemics no longer even choose whom to strike, and neither how nor when nor with what, famines and viruses and droughts and massacres and contagions and forced labor, they abound (in everything). They are already besieging the rich societies, which defend themselves the best they can, the old borders are no longer watertight. *And moreover*, in Africa and Oceania and most of Asia and the Americas. Another commonplace, and like a cloud (*some will know this light of the day after*), magnified beyond any distribution of chances and of any idea of privilege, gives rhythm to and disturbs the said phantasmal fall into the Quinary.

But if the imagination values differences, it goes back from age to age on its decisions. Today there is no longer a truly conceivable and calamitous passage between the ages, no more than the tension of the galaxies around a fatal destiny, this is what we cry out and repeat among ourselves in a sort of spell, *and in the very latest news*, even if it is still conceivable, according to the predictions of these exalted techniques which we have already praised, that a giant comet soon pulverizes the Earth or that global heating transforms it into a liquid planet, but it has stopped! We will escape from it, at least as a species, and so we wander from the thought of the apocalypse to the vocation of eternity, but listen carefully that none of the languages of the world (they have this in common that they are virtual repositories of apocalypses and dreamed sanctuaries of eternity) is in the process of becoming thicker or more brilliant or more assured than another, in truth each one quietly praises the language which is most profitable to it, and none is elected to announce the irreparable, yes catastrophes lie in wait from the bottom of the land and the sea but in the manner of secretions or of projections of our fantasies, and when they are definitive it is probable that the same subtle techniques, which are so directly applicable and so publicly chosen, will save at least a good part of the human population, and it has been said once and for all, while awaiting the next mutation of the common drive that often smolders in our imaginations and which will return to the recurrent obsessions of final extinctions. Thus, we learn to live and endure on the brink of earthquakes and massacres, even though we realize that they strike the weakest first, and we hardly wonder how this remains possible, but in the end, each from their own side, we conceive and exalt the differences between the cultures of the world now all in contact, we already know this, only we are unable to consider the realized quantity that these differences make and which would underline, for being here and there recognized, the multiplied evidence of our humanities. Equally, we in our turn become the site of an unknowable tension. And this is why, our species being tested by this future, tragic or tragedian, we love to this point the restive being, and its quantity, its totality. Poets live it, far from purities overly inspired by the philosophy of existence. And the explorers and the colonists and the conquerors and the merchants have always claimed and still intend to reduce being to the oneness of their large assets and their possessions, and thus to eradicate diversity, because they have always felt it beating in them like a damnation. The publicists of the well-equipped nations, those there and then those here who believe themselves to be responsible for the concrete of things, and for information as well as for reflection and evolution, which revolve *around the very inflation of their only variety*, and they have invented the art of communication which they do not intend sharing with whomever it might be, from another subsidized world, feel the same way, and they suffer from feeling the diversity beating within them, which they have taken in horror. For this reason, they abhor poets, either born here or coming from everywhere, who speak obscurely of the multiplicity of the world. They have hatred. It is the only hatred that matters to them, that of poetry. Could it be so with history, or the novel or the art of the essay, or the technique of making wooden dolls, here in Naples and here in Dublin, that in the same way people could not bear to consider? Yes and yes and certainly, at least in those favored countries where only a few take advantage of the leisure of such obfuscations.

If our imaginations thus flow and transform and stagnate and recede and leap suddenly, always in relation to these differences that we recognize or not between our various relations of nature and culture, we all accept on the other hand to agree that we are entering into this *new region of the world*, of totalized space, of relativized time, where everyone already admits that differences are determinant, but most often they refuse to recognize that their sum, their realized quantity, sketches another Relation, quite different because we have so long ignored it, but we know that it is made and brewed from inextricable and propitious contaminants. We refuse it, despite the fact that our places are now very open. Our places are open and they are within us and they are unchangeable, and we cannot go around them, we cannot lock them up without more in our confinements, they are promised to the visitation of the Other, this much too crazy probability that we push back once again, we see that the Other is an often idle tourist, or a reputed invader and dispossessor, so the bushes do not yet meet the deserts, and neither the Cities their borders. Thus, we stick to those sections of differences that we first raised like walls, and which resonate as so many barriers until then not permeable, which have been so harshly incarnated, peoples of nations of excess and wandering peoples and peoples floored by the geographies where they grew in vain and peoples dominated by the masters of work and peoples reduced to so slow extinction and peoples with a universal vocation and peoples so soon withdrawn into their comforts and all these solitary geologies bubbled with their single mysteries, so we raised these sections of the differences between them, but we are again and again reluctant to conceive their confluences, the international organizations that regulate us can do nothing about it and they could not find how to help us, even if they really wanted to, they do not know how to stir up imaginations or *turn the poetic ship around*, in the end their precious laws govern an infinite amount of dust, having regard to the enormous and disrupted mass of these sections that it would be a matter of spreading in patterns that could not be undone, in a moving network. And the rest of us, informal heap of the legislated, we ask ourselves indiscriminately this question that is for once truly universal and we shout it on the horizons and we do not perceive that others are shouting it with us and at the same time as *all of us*, and we suspect that there is no universal answer to this question, question and answer do not go hand in hand, how to act and concretely do justice to this entanglement? How to open and maintain justice from here and how to establish fraternity with over there? We are quietly screaming. Our voices sink into the ground without echo. *The cry is an aborted root.*

In the magmatic temple where the poets dreamed, the pillars of which are made up of so many sections of differences which await to be connected with one another, there are distributed religious recitations which borrow the appearances of art. It is the most regular object of our pleasures, right at the mouths of rivers and in television broadcasts and at the top of buildings and in the large open requisitioned spaces or in the secret of the caves of the cities or of the cinemas. Why this modelized art? Because, alone perhaps, with if the occasion permits the ceremonies of the various religions in vogue and the lively debates of the sects, and with the transports of music and the immense liturgies of sporting gatherings, which spread beyond the sound and the fury, it can bring to a degree of bearable incandescence the expression of our anxieties and our rages, the uneasiness we feel at not being able to both experience and recognize what Mr. Louis Sala-Molins would have sarcastically called our existence-ness and our being-ness. But, that kind of art? Yes. Because it is, thus conceived and agitated, an avowable pretext, and that it can cover up the troubles of the world and the unbearable gaps, and rise to delirium that which will never be called delirium, with the harsh admissibility of that which imitates the real and brags about it loudly and brags only about it. Thus closely adapted to our conditions, this art, the blockbuster films which overwhelm us in a folly of spaces and times and the television shows which imitate so well our everyday existences and its modest nature and the festival theaters, this is where there are festivals, at the annually reassuring conventions for all, and serial novels whose monotonies amaze us every time and suspense documentaries where the secrets of the universe and our lives are hunted down like criminals and the worldwide hit songs that make us change worlds in spaces this time as uniform as one another, all this beautiful art, reduced to a single semblance and to so many astonishing virtuosities, will also have turned into as many literal formulations of this thrust (toward the realized quantity of differences of the world) which we have proposed it had represented, and from the first leap into the humanities, one of the most spectacular and surreptitious manifestations of being, *insofar* as it is realized. But to remain literal is what sets the absolute limits of such an exercise nowadays. There is no longer a wall in this cave, art has entered into its own film and gets lost in it. The effort and the miracle (in art) toward any totalized quantity of differences cannot be reduced to becoming at this point repetitive of the image that we grant ourselves of the real, for example the anger and the violence, or the rhythm so totally obsessed that rescinds itself, or the simplicity that does not want to tackle the ugly complex things, the effort and the miracle in doing so only afford a partial recitation of this real. And it is precisely this lack, and let us go over it again, which was seen and defined above in our speech as the consequence of a *literal formulation*. The exasperation and the excess and the tumult and immoderation, we imagine them pulsating in the world, they are not sufficient in themselves as forms or modes of this search or of this tension toward the realization of differences, no more than did the graffiti and the derision and the monumental and the cropped language and no more than they have been, not so long ago. The main coloring of these arts which have not spread over and taken hold of the world and have not gone beyond with their techniques, arts that the nomenclatures hesitate so much to name, indigenous arts and primitive arts and distant arts and other arts and first arts, it remains that they have not exerted any secular influence in the world, of which moreover they have not reproduced any literality, as if they had from the beginning reserved their energies for the true encounter to come and for the entry into what we call this *new region of this world*. One dimension watches over the principle of the tension of art, which is at the heart of the growth of differences and which signals beauty, it is that of the poetic intention, which animates all the practices of art, whether we gathered it by dint of swarf, whether it was first given to a few, either in pure science or in innocence, like an imposition of lightning. The poetic intention has always led to the absolute prescience of the Whole-World. Any poetic intention leads from the outset to a narrative of the world, for which this narrative is not narrative, but a state of the relation of the differences between them in a surrounding, narrow or expanding, it depends, and in a given time. So it is with the presence of landscapes when, recognizing ourselves in the situation of our open and unavoidable places, we hear the song of the world. The colors of the landscapes enter into our spoken words and our gestures, and here it is then that these landscapes suddenly relate to and know one another. They can be tumultuous and excessive as much as shy, gentle, or light. There will be no idealism in declaring that the voice of the deserts confronts and prolongs the song of the rains, which are lacking there and suffocate us here. And declared idealism is in fact the revelation of the energy currents which link our differences together. But this could just as well be a poetic approach to any materialism, from the dogmatic Leucippus to the very nuanced Cheikh Anta Diop. The landscapes of the world release energy, which is not even at rest, it is primarily that of all these differences, manifested there. And the voiceless peoples, which we called peoples without writing, it's the same thing and they are the same, we have said so. It is not, however, true that these people without audible voice would benefit from a power, for example of truth, because of these depths from which their voice was to rise. Poor living, you understand, has never procured privilege. Those who profit from such a power, but the latter does not partake of the truth, it is above all because they hold the rare powers of the techniques, but some infirmity comes to them also from the way such privilege hides the world from them, as it is and where it is going. This world that they scrutinize and control and that they are so eager to dominate. The powers of techniques, if only for a moment, no longer generate big ideas, neither grand ideas, nor those astonishing sharp general theories which derive from knowledge and imagination, these techniques are exhausted today in the joyful microscopies of their established systems which unfold in full force, the triumphant and anxious technicians may conceive and accept differences, it is true, but they push back at all costs to consider the relation between these differences, this is Relation, and the fully realized quantity at the end of all the diversities. Yes, differences lead directly to diversity. But at the end? Would there be an end to this possible quantity of differences, to the realization of this quantity in total? A sinister proposition, which would evoke a world put into a stupendous immobilization, and which no force would ever be able to move. But for us, *and for all of us*, this so-called *fully realized amount of differences* has meant first and only that none of the differences in the world will be put aside or kept apart. And we enter into the Whole-World, which always for us covers the totality of the world, but here it is that this Whole-World is also in our actuality *another region of the world*, a whole new region, and the world is there, it is right-here, it is ahead of us, who say it without saying it while saying it again, undertaking a new category of literature. None of the regions of the world is really unknown, the explorers have driven their trains to their endpoint, yet there is *another region of the world* in the world, which we have not traveled so much, for we will have to cross it all together, it is this very improbable Whole-World, and *a few had knowledge of it*. Well then, the world is completely recognized, and the Whole-World covers entirely the world, however and for us the Whole-World is to be discovered and known. It is a part of the world, which right-here transcends the world and designates it. The world is the known and the Whole-World the unknown, but the opposite is just as true, and again, the world is the whole and the Whole-World the part, but the reverse speaks to us as much. We will always have had the unknown world in front of us and we will be able to dream of it, alone or not, and also, always the Whole-World in us and next to us, that we will share but with all. And the differences in turn derive from other differences, each of them based not only on a variety or an identity but also on the gap that rushes in, like a bridge, from this variety to all the others, and these generated differences together produce, beyond diversity, the unpredictable continuity of the world. Relation does not recognize any border, neither in space nor in time, yet we need the borders. But it is because Relation is the fundamental border, which is the open passage. It appears to us then that the peoples without audible voice for such a long time have filled this space and bridged this gap of all variety to all the others, but not by encumbering the gap with their own fixities, and that they have maintained there the thought of the dreamed, or realized quantity. This was not a way to elect oneself. If there were human communities to travel from one entanglement of Relation to another, they then gave the explorers and the conquerors and the untrammeled exploiters, by and in the full pillaging of the cities and the bloody labor of the slave and the intense slaving ports and the sealed heavy plantations and the Latifundia where to get lost and in the floods of the metropolises and for the races around the world and the pogroms and the pleasures of the techniques and the aristocracy of the discoveries and the wars of religions and in the weapons of total destruction and the obscurations of the planet Earth, there appeared others, or rather they did not make themselves visible, to support on the contrary, also obscurely, and closely, the gap, the signifying margin, they did not move from their given place, yes and they fought one another but they also maintained themselves in the inextricable thickness, it was their way of continuing the complicity, so that at the moment where they all entered into this *new region of the world* that we are entering into, the varieties or the identities of the peoples without exception and of their surroundings (in all) are neither lost nor distorted nor locked in excess, and that finally the differences come together, and here opposing and there generating another beauty. And immediately the common feeling decrees squarely that it was neither a vocation nor a mission, much less a right, of these *dwelling* peoples, that the histories and futures of the humanities are not decreed in advance nor once and for all, that it happened like that, that is all. There were peoples who undertook to run with the foolish techniques of the world, and it itched them to death to roam the nooks and crannies of the horizons, and other peoples who put up with maintaining the difficult contiguities of this same world, and that was all. Divergences which are at the source of *all of us*, now that these peoples really encounter each other. *Nature is a temple*, as much to specify a unity-diversity, another common site, and we conceive it thus, and the works of art are it too, temple and place and diversity, and the small rocks buried on the riverbanks, too, which Nature seems to have forgotten. The most discreet waters and the humblest lands. Poetry is the only narrative of the world and it discerns these presences and it adds to the landscapes and it reveals and connects the diversities and it foretells and names these differences and it opens for so long onto our consciousness and it revives our intuitions. Throughout this time which concerns us and passes for us, poetry designates and accomplishes that quantity (of the differences) which is realized and which provides the movement and gives life to the unfinishable and the unexpected.

Most of the ideas of difference have regarded it as just what separates, the gap, and what initially invites, the relation or the alliance, and perhaps that which links and relays and connects also, Relation. Such is the case with Segalen, one of the most generous founding figures of difference, and with Deleuze, the imperceptible diffuser. Difference acts passively or exalts, in every case it is considered as the mediation of two substances, or of two or several varieties, or of an infinity of identities, or else as the sole motor or the hoist or the balance of a central process, strange to itself, and these thoughts almost never envisage it as a substance itself, or as a constituent of being, or as what we would call a technical language or as *source data*. That is, however, what it is, for the reason that a completely passive function, or a neutral gap, to which one would reduce it in considering it as a simple mediation, could not have influenced components as infinite as the varieties or the identities, either to postpone them or to immobilize them or to bring them together. Neither life nor its hidden or obvious forms are engagements. Differences, which palpitate to the secret of beauty, of work or of object, could not have fulfilled the vow to complete this or that object, river or mountain or cast bronze or idea or passion or song, and they could not have played this game of negotiations-attractions, if they were not themselves and first of all living realities, changing and saved from the dull ticktock of the machine. Techniques and performances, manual and intellectual, as much as the action of Nature, which allow to identify the form of a work of art or the appearance of an object, are neutral if they are found, only move because they are moved, but it is indeed the aggregation of the said form or of the aforementioned appearance which gradually brings, in the form and in the appearance, in and through them, a place where the circus of the world is played and where all tragedy is exhausted and where ancient differences take shape and where stir already those differences to come, this place of nascent beauty, and we recognize that these are not mechanisms, and that their association, and their congress, either in the work or in the object, secrete by fusion and designate by effusion, beauty, the heralding figure. It is this force which itself pronounces itself, and of itself protects its own fragility.

We are surprised by this idea, which has always wandered around but which we have maintained with a beautiful laziness, that after all we have no sure indication about the variety, or the identity, of these cave people who had so originally tried to surprise the secret of effusion and connivance, Plato may have reinvested the cave and dared *to change* what was on the wall, mixing in it the lure of the real and the divination of light, yet we are no better equipped to ratify the origin or the descent of these peoples, at least in complete certainty, and perhaps we never will be, nor to certify which parts of humanity today have inherited the experience of fusion and the taste of this connivance, its memory or its trace, or if we all *follow on* from it together, or if we all forget it together, there is an obvious missing link, and this idea that the idea of filiation itself is already shaky, in this starting point of all the stories. Are we the consecrated descendants, that you would deem legitimate, of the strongest of these clan leaders, or the clandestine offspring, in other words bastards, of these artists, themselves protected by women, melted into the troop and scorned by the others, who nevertheless consented to their miracles exhibited in stone? Everything is in everything. Let us consider together that, in our actuality, the most derisory forms of human expressions and the most appalling acts of stupidity or of our belittlement and the most unrelenting and most spectacular playfulness of our anxieties of having to live here together, and the most complacent aberrations to which the minutiae of techniques lead, or moreover, and on the other side, the most reductive mimicries of folkloric shows, said to be bound to our authenticity or the most stupid bragging grown from our obvious desires for revenge or justice, for those who have suffered so much from the misfortunes of history, can take as legitimate a place in the inextricable part of this world as the thick processions of probabilities or that the heavy mess of intuitions where we sink more often when we meditate on our places and our histories, *all of us*, and our cries, as in this very discourse. In the end of everything, fiction and narrative will have the leisure to parade their trivialized versions, and the denials of poetry, to fully release their detestations. We are perhaps not very distant from the time where inconceivable forms and new genres of art, that are unsuspected today, will reveal to us the rendezvous of differences and the other secrets of magnetic connections. Or perhaps the walls of our future caves will be glittering, blindingly empty glass facades without a breath of air nor echo, and these caves themselves space stations suspended haphazardly in rarefied imaginations, where we could project neither fusion nor vow of connivance. The traces and the magnetic connections would all vanish, this would be the real apocalypse, from which no one escapes. But no need to predict in this way, and let us leave poetry to poetry. Who will see will say. The road alone knows the secret.

The secret of difference is that it is the first to manage the variations of identity, in other words, the variety of the living. It is certainly not the same and the other, nor their agreement, which weave Relation, it is the different, which animates the leaps and the bounds of the Whole-World and allows the same and the other to be. However, the most pernicious calamities of the racist impulse are exercised first against the nuances of difference rather than against the radicalities of alterity, of otherness. The Nazi ghetto is more resolute in this sense than the townships of apartheid. For fascist thought, it is not the other that alters and threatens (it would occur for example in the vicinity of a Japanese or a Masai, so radically other) but above all the *different in the same*, and what the racist hates the most is the mixture that introduces nuance and variation. This racist will get into a group to kill negroes, straight out, even if he has traded and profited from them as a priority, this racism is above all a justification for exploitation, but if the racist is white and Nazi, he will torture infinitely homosexuals, the mentally ill, Gypsies, Slavs, and in the first place Jews, because they suggest to him so unbearably that they are very close to him. He burns books, because they remind him that these Jews, who are a priori indistinguishable (the star is required) think and create as much and more than himself. One of the racist's surest boastings will be the ability he claims to be able to recognize a Jew anywhere, and at first glance. In this way he reassures himself against the imperceptible difference and believes he is assured of an insurmountable differentiation. The excesses of ferocity of a significant part of the whites of the South of the United States toward the black populations of these same regions undoubtedly arose from the whites' secret rage at resembling in so many ways those whose animality they claimed in order to better justify slavery. It is possible that the Hutu and then Tutsi killers displayed much more ferocity among themselves and against their populations than they would have practiced against the white settlers during an anti-colonial insurgency. We have seen how, in the countries of immigration, recent generations of immigrants are the most intolerant of recent arrivals, their peers in every way. And the most effective disposition to disarm racism is indeed not the exaltation of a universalist humanism whose moralities always remain without concrete effect nor the apology of a persecuted race, whatever pain and demand for justice that we feel in the face of genocides and holocausts, but the song of consented difference, that is to say of coming together, mixing and creolization, which terrify the racist, whose fundamentalist way of thinking loathes the perditions, which it imagines for itself. Now it is difference, and not the identical, which is the elementary particle of the relational fabric. There, identities are kept preserved from dilutions, how could a difference in fact demand a difference if it is already perverted by a domination which it could not resist, and thus, to conclude, domination and integration and dilution and mimicry and imitation and assimilation are outside the field of Relation, they only appear in it in the manner of brakes, and equally the identities that are the most sure of themselves are at the same time magnetized from one change and from one exchange with the other. The differences weave and play in what is safe, so they change it, without losing or distorting it. Whoever is not sure of their identity fears above all to subject their identity to such nuanced relationships and to *expose* it to differences. Such is the lot of the racist.

Difference concerns both varieties and identities, in short, the substance of things, but also the way of conceiving and presenting them, a forecast of their structures and an account of their arrangement, in other words, an aesthetic. Difference partakes of all the substances, and also manifests concern for their placing and their arrangement, the integral relation of the parts to the whole. Aesthetics have often tried to be the difficult science of this inextricability, but the humanities have alas become numb in their unthinking ignorance of these aesthetics which each time tried to recognize connivance and to find the secret of the magnetic connections, and we have denied until today that they designate one of the foundations of knowledge. We discover that there are at least two qualities of differences, which in fact are differents, that which each variety claims for itself in order to constitute itself into a variety, and that of which each variety takes charge in order to vary precisely and thereby conform to its nature. If the substance is known to be changing, it is indeed difference which causes the substance to *remain* while changing. We know this, yet we persist in ignoring it. A function which would not come under physical science or mathematics or the suddenly so-called human sciences, but of this too little-known aesthetic, which precedes all aesthetics of the beautiful, and which designates in the matter and in the mind and in the imaginations and fantasies of peoples and in any aptitude for beauty, the primordial work of differences, precisely. Beauty is the sign of what, there, is *going to change*. Now, through the too tormented designs of such an aesthetic, what differences can we find between difference and the different?

We must not be troubled by the futile, pedantic and smug character of the declaration that should be made about the different, and which marks only the multifaceted complexity of the question we are dealing with. *The different is not that which differs, or which has differed, but that which, added to the other, or proposed to the other, and coming from the same, constitutes an other of the other or a variety of the same, and who is no longer either the other or the same, without, however, ceasing to be the other, and consequently, and for oneself, the same.* The substance varies, without ceasing to be itself. To be oneself. We are relieved to have crossed the threshold of this formulation, like a panting that never ends, and to come to what we can deduce from it. Difference is the operative force of the movement of varieties and identities, which causes them to constitute themselves, and the different is that which by such a movement varies from one variety to another, and becomes more precise from one identity to the other, or rather causes varieties and identities to vary without being distorted, and thus contributes to forming the fabric of the living and its relationship to its surroundings. This is why we say *indifferently* one for the other, and difference and the different, proving the substance by its movement. And it is wrong that we believe of a variety or an identity that they are different, they are other, having incorporated differences that have changed them without distorting them. It is also a chimera to lay foundations on the preeminence of a variety or of an identity, for the moving tissue of the differents is a rhizome, from which grows neither a root which kills all around nor a trunk which subjugates. These radical emergences were the consequence of the very steps taken by the human spirit in its quest for rootedness and security, at the time when communities-nations were being built and peoples-States were established. We cannot, however, conclude that the rhizome is a pure avatar or a prototype of flatness, or of immobility or of the static thing, its infinite variety unfolds in the expanse rolled up on itself, and under all directions, by a non-linear multi-force, then its eminences as much as its depths are exchanged in permanent movement in our spaces. The peak and the abyss, the tops and the bottoms, and the single root and the dominant trunk, variables integrated into this expanse, are physical realities whose meaning had been projected by the human mind, which interpreted in that way the diversities of the universe. The top and the bottom, and the near and far, will very soon no longer be for us suitable frameworks for our encounter with the world. We enter fully into the imaginaries of circularity or spirality, the latter being dear to Mr. Franketienne. That is to say that our places, both terrestrial and marine, remain at the same time centers and peripheries, and that the vertigo that grows there, maelstrom abyss leviathan, or the high trees which rise there, sequoias and mahoganies and oaks and pear trees and casuarinas and solar yews and acacias and flamboyants and acomas, no longer dominate there.

OUR WANDERINGS, EITHER IN
DEFTNESS OF RECEIVED IDEAS OR IN
DISCOMFORT OF THE SITUATIONS,
FOLLOW NEITHER A DISORDER NOR
AN ORDER, BUT TRACES.

The common-places, with a hyphen, as we have repeated so often would be localities and ideas and feelings and sites and engagements and imaginaries and dreams and information and manifestos—where already a thought of the world has met a thought of the world, support for us the best possible guarantees against the void and the unjust and the silliness and the semblance of commonplaces, without a hyphen, these reservoirs of all the false evidences by which governments dumbfound public opinion, and false truths by which the clerks persuade naive people to believe in the simplified logics and excellences of the universe and of human societies which would come to please their clergy, and we are naive bodies, more or less all of us: who could argue the opposite? The common-place gives us the intuition of the Whole-World, the commonplace, without a hyphen, is also necessary for us, to recapitulate the histories of the world, and we have used it broadly here, because it is indeed the repetition of evidences which helps to enter into the inextricable. The power of this hyphen, however, which reforms the vulgar and the banal and the shriveled of this common here, and transmutes it, and constitutes it in depositary and in a brilliant unifier of this common here. We are then susceptible to the sensational variations of the language that we put into practice, whether it is made of excessively dazzling ruptures or long continuities, and without our having sought it or having really achieved mastery of it, there is the whole accident of writing or declamation, but rather, depending on whether we have also deduced it from this spoken-written language which is our own, which we adopted,

or whether we invented it from of our sung-spoken language, we will see
later how the latter can become spoken-written but also quite conversely
how a spoken-written language could become again sung-spoken, or even
from these two at the same time, or soon from several languages at the
same time, or starting from everything and nothing at the same time, and
in this circumstance we build dizzying sectors of differences, stretched by
words and speeches, *the cry is a rhizome*, which oppose and agree with an
equal astonishment, or depending on whether, finding us weary from a very
personal and already ancient energy, far removed from the energies of the
world, we descend the flow of this low-parlance which, in so much sudden
crashing, pulls us slowly and with fragility.

The *langages* of painters and sculptors, architects and musicians, as well
as philosophers, are of the same kind. And ideas and forms, colors and
spaces, will be a question of bringing excess to its own moderation and
to affix a writing to its orality or vice versa and perhaps inventing beyond
these categories, to rejoin as many sectors of differences that were already
rising to a *realized* quantity. Why moderation and excess and writing and
orality, if not that the Earth by turning on itself thus gave birth to them.
The rhythms of matter, echoes of the voice, these are the human manifestos
of difference, and which bind us to the elements. Perhaps these couples also
govern the pathways of the arts linked to the sciences or of the sciences
that verge on art? There is a hidden orality of the plastic arts, see the works
of Haitian peasant painting, and the elementary nature of the color, the
cut-up symbolism of the lexical forms, and the repetition of statures and
the accumulation that fills the canvas without any perspective and without
emptiness *below or behind*, and the assonances of the Creole language which
resound there, and I would hazard to say that orality marks the paintings
before the invention of perspective, which represented the line of writing
that goes toward infinity, and there is also a falsely improvised language
of architecture, thus the non-atavistic but enrooted emergence of Brasilia,
and the attempt at a measure of excess in these capitals of the newly rich
countries, erected monstrously in a stroke and all completed before being
populated, which become ghost towns before coming alive, or conversely,
the recommencements of lakeside cities, inhabited at the very moment that
they are already withering along with their yellowing, so frail reeds, all
seasonal oralities which are expressed softly and swiftly, by naive glass and
cement or by innocent leafing, and there is a secret measure of the forms
of music and philosophy, also, the two arts closest both in their precision
and by their evanescence, a measure which radiates from the scattering
and from the violence of their materials, that is to say from their hidden

excess, and everywhere in these arts a new way of suspense and encounter, yes a suspense of the world, and a panting, evenly tuned to the regular depth of our breaths as much as to the disorderly tortures of the living. The same panting that catches us in these caves. And the architectures that we call natural, gullies and springs and mountain ridges, punctuate these unexpected breaths. There, all the differences of the world meet one another infinitely, and idealism and materialism, which formerly opposed their axioms, have now only rhetorical rigor, and no longer any reason to curse each other.

La Cohée du Lamentin … What in splendor was already a place of places, a corner of the seaside where we bathed, me as timoune, and a tiny sign of the country, connecting it to the so quivering spawning of the world. There, the word *cohée* is full of the sparkling of the sun, and it is also obscured by that brightness. Is its origin ubiquitous, or completely French, but we do not find a trace of it in the lexicons, or really Creole, but this language has such a prodigious art of camouflaging its creations with words, and finally, do the various meanings of this speech-word *cohée* meet? I said I had heard of a Fond-cohé in Saint-Pierre, but I read on a map of this region Fond-Corré. A friend from Guadeloupe tells me that a cohé is a bird of the seaside, it glides over the shores with its beak open, to swallow up mosquitoes and all other flying insects without landing. In such an unstable and perhaps distressing situation, it cries out, and its cry, it is said, announces sudden deaths, but it is doubtless said because this cry spreads like a loud, mysterious tearing that in my turn and for some time I thought I heard. The particularity is that the Creole word of this term does not take, as it should in this language, either masculine or feminine, whereas the French word goes from one to the other. *Un* cohé or *une* cohée, but *an* cohé is always *an* cohé, which is not more masculine than neuter or feminine. A strange vocation for such a secret part of a sea bay. See also that this cohé, when we project it in the inverted mirror, Mr. Pascal G. pleasantly points out to me, suggests an echo to us, at least in a designated disorder. This cohée of Lamentin is for me what the traces of childhood project into each of us to teach us the Whole-World. The variants of such an obscure term, cohée, also correspond to our common ways of dealing with diversities, the echoes of which most often were buried first in some cave of time, with walls overloaded with uncertain glimmers, where lie darkened flickers of former connivances, before resounding sharply over the expanses and showing us the parades of the beautiful. I see then that the echo and the cohée force me to recognize in myself the instinct for the border.

The intuitive acquaintance with the sea, which at first seemed unspoiled from all borders, is endless, and even from the deepest depths of the land and the cities. The pioneers of the American Far West, at the end of their fantastic crossing of the continent, were suddenly *floored* from having reached the sea, the Pacific Ocean, whose power they had imagined so much and then so underestimated. The seas, right at the forefront of the human wanderings, always postpone borders and horizons, they allow communication, that is to say, to commute, and it is through this they soon ravage the heart. As for the cities, they rise in flashes in deserts of cement and glass, we do not know the new materials born of the technique, and then they flow with an imperceptible movement, like a cat which stretches in its dream, they dig into the misery which in turn buries them in the dust and mud of sparse lands. Happy is he who lays out his city at leisure. All these countries riddled with shanty towns and cardboard houses and collapsed streets. And then in the distance, these countrysides without countryside and these forests without forest and these villages without village and these roads without road. Between commonplaces and common-places, which have provided the occasion and often the subject matter of this work, we found the distance, signed with a hyphen, and we underlined another partition (a debased place, a shared place) from one to the other of outbuildings, with so outdated functions, it is now high time to question the places. To recite them at sea and to draw their borders, which are dug into the sea, it is not preserved from them, it rolls them in its swells, it feeds on them, which are not limits, but the now permeable passages where every difference seeks every difference.

What would it be like to "enter the real," as we have repeatedly proposed? Will it be a building into which we enter and from which we leave at will? One thing, open or closed? A phenomenon apart from the world and apart from life? And, as for us, are we going to a place of unreality, which would be filled somehow with the content of these too hazy reals? But too vain and scandalous these questions, faced with the calm terror of the world, and the distress of children. If I say, speaking narrowly from my assumptions and in my own name, as one must also get used to, that art thus enters the real, it is because I conceive the moment when the realizable quantity of the differences that pulsates in each work of art, and the tension of this same work toward all or part of the differences around, begin to be perceived (but not as an unheard of quality), and first of all by the artist, deliberate or not, at this moment when the work is still only a project of relations between all kinds of differences which concern it, then by the spectator who, recognizing this tension and these encounters in the vicinity of the beauty of the work, completed or not, instinctively constitutes them (with this work) in relay elements in what it imagines to be the quantity realized of the differences of the world. It is thus with all the works born of the desire, of the judgment or of the madness of the humanities, and for the works of Nature, and equally for the constructs of thought, and for the destruction propagated by men, and for the catastrophes littered everywhere still by Nature, and for the changes and leaps of the imaginary, when they leave traces right-here, and for the tapped traces of the sufferings of peoples, and also for the bottomless oblivion of the sufferings of abandoned peoples, and for the joys which often cover these torments. Thus, the work of art really enters into the realized quantity of the differences of the world, it is the marker of their meetings, of their Relation. A horse painted on the rock of a cave by an artist who has not signed the work, or engaged in battle by an Italian craftsman of the fourteenth or fifteenth centuries, and no doubt Caravaggio, or carved in the shape of a royal seat by a Berber blacksmith who did not leave a name, or dismembered in the tumult of a massacre by Picasso. This tension toward a result of the differences, which change each time, predicting an encounter. The diversions (of this horse for example, but it could have been any acoma or fetish or sand lizard or damsel in the bath, the motifs that meet are not for real, but are the most often illegal laws of magnetic connection) send back to each other the image of the quantity dreamed, realized. But if the works of art thus teach us to relate all beauty to a repetition and to an accumulation and to a sense of permanence and to a feeling of eternity, other phenomena or other workings of real life lead us to entrust it to what seems temporary to us and fleeting to such a point that it forces us to hasten in our turn to join up with it. The flash of a song and the density of a rainfall and the wind of an inferno and the sinking bed of a cart of mad sands. When it is not the fleeting transparency of a barely known impression or of an idea barely born. And today, in art, some still try to join this fleetingness, by works skillfully disposed to the ephemeral, but such works would rather make us despair, forcing us to remember that works of beauty above all demand permanence, so that they can best indicate to us the certain moment when nothing will be forgotten or disappointed by the varieties of the humanities. And Nature alone seems to us to have the right to confess or to exercise the ephemeral, because it alone maintains and sustains an irrefutable course of things. For the humanities, they do *real* work each time they add to the realized quantity of differences, they do so for example by conceiving and illustrating the idea of the achievable totality of this dreamed quantity, and each time also that they relate to it their own varieties or identities, kept whole and open. We mean by this that the world is the place where differences are accentuated, as one would point out to you that the features of a face are pronounced, and that the Whole-World, contemporary with the world, is the place where these same differences mutually acquit each other, are conceived at the end and are received. To enter into the real, is perhaps to feel to the highest degree these encounters, or these revealing simultaneities. Works of art thus read or elect the world, but with the same impetus and at the same time as they predict the Whole-World. There was never any pure absolute self-sufficiency of the imagination, in a Whole-World which would have been outside the world, nor was there any unidirectional realism, branding a neutral world, soon weaned off the unforeseen events of a Whole-World.

Our places are perhaps not only the sites that we frequent and name, or that we literally create, but also the traces from which we clear the grass, and the obscure ideas that we unravel without striking them with transparencies, and the common-places, where we have encountered formulations from afar or images appearing in other languages. The places that we knew yesterday intertwine in solidarity and they weave a baroque text, as the sea waters know how to do, about which we have to decide if it supports what we would call our identity, or if it is us that give the density to the text that engages each of the said places further each time in the support of its landscape. A difficult and grainy text, that twinges repeatedly like sea waves around one of these rocks which punctuate the coasts of the world. And a text broken free from new beginnings, and which in turn seems to make possible the reality of as many borders as there are waves there. We do not consent to frequenting any places except on the basis of the praise, the eulogies, that we give them. And an indifferent place, or a place that rejects you, does not suit our cosmic sense of duration, the flash of their revelation immediately vanishes, the inconvenience and the displeasure they bring do not hold, and it is because we unconsciously or suddenly reject the idea or the taste that there could be forbidden or evil places. We tend not to believe in the Underworld, and the balanced view of Purgatory, if we were religious, would satisfy us well. The praise of a Heaven, by consequence, would seem to us to reproduce too much the abomination of a Hell. From then on, the places that will have nourished our imaginations, we can only consider them as Splendors, without morality or merit. Because the aesthetics of the world do not give birth to any ethics which in turn would constrain them. The measure or the excess of beauty is enough to endow it with meaning and with what we call "value." Let us see then the unnamable place of the slave ship, this absolute of annihilation, and how today we recompose it? We derive lessons from it, and perhaps reasons to hope or to undertake, and bets on what will happen to us, but for those who suffered it, and who soak forever in its infernal rot, there was only that, that is to say the annihilation, and the revolts that they raised there aimed only at that, to retreat at full force from annihilation. The border between them and us, who raise the memory, remains marked by this irreparable absolute of the lived. But it is a border, however, and which like any border is permeable, at least in our poetics, and we need its mark, so that the memory or the forgetting are shared by all. We need the imperceptible weft to cross, which passes from one variety of the world to another, and transfigures difficult memory into knowledge that is finally bearable. Thus, this border is what unites.

The ability to transform our places of suffering or defeat into places of promise, even when it would be too easy to substitute ourselves for those who really suffered defeat and tears, will allow us to cross the border with places where other humanities suffered and endured, and to conceive of these places in praise and splendor. As for the legal borders between the communities, let us observe how pleasant it is to cross them without constraint, without restraint, to continue as naturally from the Moroccan ambiance to the Algerian ambiance, and from this living-France to this living-Spain, and from the air that we breathe in Savoy to the air that we breathe in Tuscany ("Tuscany is still far away?"), and from the blue deserts of Peru to the ocher deserts of Chile, you feel incredibly light as if you were wearing some strange clothing, and full of an ancient appetite for what is to come, the border is this invitation to taste the differences, and a total pleasure to vary, but then let us come back to all those who do not have such a leisure, the forbidden immigrants, and imagine the terrible weight of this prohibition. Crossing the border is a privilege which no moun or timoune should be deprived of, for whatever reason. There is no border except for this plenitude to at last go beyond it, and *through it*, to fully share in the pure differences. The obligation to have to force whatever border it may be, under the pressure of poverty, is as scandalous as are the very foundations of this misery. This is why the Ports, slavers or not, touch us so much.

Philosophy is an art, and it is difficult to define it, for the reason that no one first admits this quality. Philosophy does not call for truth, it brings together the truths of the world to designate beauty, thus the concepts and the intuitions and the practice of ruptures and connections are its materials, and if the beautiful is the splendor of the true, they are the accepted truths which signal the meeting of differences, beauty is incessantly there. Beauty belongs to aesthetics, beauty is given or revealed in a vision of the world. There are specialists in aesthetics, but the vision of the world arises from the gaze of the artist, whether he is an artist or a philosopher or a scholar or even a man of action, as they say. Whether they be systematic or prudent. So, the scholar or the historian or the man of action or the good naturalist can be mistaken, and in their systems Darwin can be mistaken, and Hegel be mistaken, and Gibbon can be mistaken, and Che Guevara be mistaken again, so all of them, but their overall visions tremble and do not falter. When we said that formerly aesthetics preceded ethics, we were mistaken only about a stage to go through or a meaning to complete. As exuberant as it may seem to assert, the gesture of the person in the caves who paints the animal and its surroundings proceeds from an impossible vision of the world, and not from an instinct and even less from a convention, and it is then the taking possession of this environment, and consequently the appearance of utilitarian art, which in the end will decide on the rules as aesthetics progressively improve, a science of the beautiful, as they will do with the rules of techniques, the practical sciences of action. These prescriptions will be erected into absolute general laws of universal value and, for all we know, there where the norms of creation in most cultures of the world will have rather been lived and supported and considered as a collection of taboos and prohibitions. And then see that the so-called universal law is much more restrictive than the particular taboo. A vision of the world, which is outside any system, from one side to the other of all the seas integrates aesthetic and technical laws, and taboos, but it can equally ignore them. We find ourselves on the shores of these seas, fully ready for this encounter, already assumed or granted in the first artistic gesture and intuition from the time of the caves, between paintings and representations, these finished objects of so-called civilized cultures, and these others, that so many studies bring together without really distinguishing them or quite bringing them together, and that Apollinaire at the beginning of the twentieth century still miscalled his "Fetishes of Oceania."

At the time of my childhood, Apocal and Fetnat were inseparable, as it often happened for people crushed by the quiet misery of their surroundings, and who found in wandering companionship the subtle principle of resistance to misfortunes. Cane cutters during the season and when the inconveniences of life pushed them to it, and most of the time picking up the odd informal job, they were also the voice that cried out for everyone; and everyone, even the timoune that I was, seemed to realize it. There, *the cry was the fiery consciousness of the sun*, even though it was the rainy season, and Apocal and Fetnat cried out for all, even though they drifted silently into a flurry of patronal festivals. I tried to mark their memory in a quite unconventional book, *Malemort*, and it is true that we no longer come across these systems of association, as of Dlan Médellus Silacier, other torrid teachers that I happened to know, we all became here such normal people, at least on the surface. The sun regulated these worries of existence. Apocal had been born, one might say, on the crazy day of the apocalypse, the date of which would be difficult for you to find in the Post Office calendar, and for Fetnat it was much more natural, he was born on the day of the National Holiday, which was thus July 14 of any year. But this Apocal was not the other official Apocal, whom we will perhaps evoke one day, who kept his denomination secret, except from a few, while the simulacrum, and replica of Fetnat, spread it in his boastful moments that his name gave him access to everywhere all around. In particular, they were the unreplaced acolytes of the mayor, Mr. Otoune, in his election ceremonies, on blessed polling days. And all these extreme displays, and these lanky excitations of body and speech, and these very obscure and inalienable truths, made it that one day I was struck in my turn with an absolute revelation, and which was that Apocal and Fetnat, these debris of congruity, these unsuspected tare weights of the street scales, were in truth revisitations and reincarnations of what I would have designated under the names of existence and being, as I had learned very recently, and in a way that was probably so rudimentary, and even before knowing closely Delphi and Vernazza and the majestic desolation of the Tremiti Islands, lessons that were at the same time philosophical, Latin, and Mediterranean. But existence and being cannot be taught. Yes, the masters of the past and to come would have shuddered at the heretical character of such an assemblage. I did not disarm, I found in the dreamed and undulating delirium, and as if floating in the clouds, of Apocal, and which reminded me of those of the old Dlan the visited, and also in the clear, prosaic, and definitive declarations of this same Apocal, he was then a completely different person in other circumstances, the same certainty of knowledge and also the same satisfaction of this implied knowledge which has not to be proved or denied, and which were marks of existence, as there was in the surges of Fetnat, so close to those of Médellus and Silacier, an instinctive ruse of this same knowledge still, and an irrepressible incli- nation to relativize having and knowing everything, and without ever calculating the small possible benefits, and a fractal pleasure in designating reality in a raw and irreversible way, which were specific to being, at least I calculated it thus, and which made it that, both of them, that I understood, in the frequentation of these two wanderers, or of these three-in-one who thus dragged around the "malemort," and better than in any promise of meditation, which this existence and this being had been able to designate. All philosophy is an art, Apocal and Fetnat conceived visions of the world, of which they disdained to make a convincing exposition, and who agreed as they opposed each other.

The scattering of trails of rocks, like swirls of foam on the shores of any seas in the world, and their indefatigable repetition. And no less indefatigable, the pain and the sufferings of the peoples, the excesses of which cannot be glossed over. Which means that we suddenly practiced the art of traces, not to pick them up on our paths as we see in westerns that the scouts of the American armies did so well, but rather to invent them in ourselves and recommence the act of the maroons who left traces invisible to the eyes of their pursuers, traces which offended neither the forest nor the mountain, and which they found when they needed to. Our truths do not arise from blind clarity nor from peremptory predictions nor from mechanized systems, we will have strength in the inextricable and the upheavals of the world to advance toward these high places of the tremor that we have always frequented, for so short a time, to dare to bring together there our fetishes which are not and our fetishes which truly are, and to find these legendary *magnetic connections*, which we know they have always tempted us with, and these other *magnetic traces* by which we tried in poetry and today in all the arts to approach them or to find them. So, for us, knowledge, as it is with emotion, or like any revelation of beauty, is above all a trace. Philosophy and the other arts discover and read traces, and sometimes deposit new ones. Poetry brings them together and foretells them endlessly. The basic sciences now wish to represent and interpret them.

ONLY DIFFERENCE WOULD BE
UNIVERSAL, AND IT IS SO ONLY
THROUGH THE PLAY OF DIFFERENTS,
AND ALL IDENTITY WOULD PRIMARILY
BE BUT A MEANS OF REACHING OUT
TOWARD THE OTHER.

The unconscious awareness that we will acquire from the play of differences allows us to catch their tension in the middle of a work of art or an object. We feel that the realized quantity, to which such a work contributes, will never be accomplished, and that the beauty of this work and of any work of art is not determined or limited by any assignable end. The tension is attached to the differences manifested by the landscapes and the colors of the countries and by the nuances and the bottomless depth of their expanses, but we have not learned to relate their beauty to a single and same dimension, where the here and the other part would be given in a single part, in the right-here. The diversity of the countries offends in our eyes the familiarity of their relations, and the dialectic was taught to us precisely so that we could understand, that is to say take together, the other and the same and the outside and the inside and the other part and the right here, always for the reason that for us they did not come out of this one and the same dimension. Many peoples of the world do not keep the same and the other as separate entities, and these peoples have not needed the reparative art of dialectics. Just as, in the perception and in the representation of their worlds, these same peoples have never invented the recourse to the finer points of perspective, which is a response to an intellectual progress, and as such the development of the dialectic has called into question a technical progress. But Giotto reads the world as does the Aztec or Inca sculptor. The dialectic rallies and perspective relates that which was not given in a single movement in the sensibility or the imagination of the peoples or communities who have rallied and related the world, who had thus taken charge of manifesting the differences of the world, which they often reduced to their own unanimity, but without having planned, however, to accompany the workings-attractions of these differences.

Suddenly the idea arises that sculpture as an art has always resisted our considerations, whether it comes from here or from there, from the various coasts of the seas. As if, unlike the arts of painting, poetry, music, architecture, or philosophy, it had stood on the fringes of the debates over perspective and of the squabbles over dialectics or of the quarrel regarding questions of difference. The sculptors of the world, and those to come from the Whole-World, are arguably the closest artists to each other, and the most willing to mix their genres without giving up their styles. Let us observe how ill-suited and enlightening at the same time, in Western cultures, are the paintings of the sculptors and the sculptures of the painters. But I am more or less sure that sculptors from the banks of the Rhine, the Volga and the Congo would establish corresponding lexicons. Perhaps this is because, and even for those who work with wood, or cardboard, or breadcrumbs, or intractable marble, or scrap, or of course steel with its bitter taste, the memory of fire, of which the only blacksmith was the obscure master, remains the common-place. Fire is one of the paths of metamorphosis, this very elevated site of agreed differences. And the sculptor forges not only the form but the space around, there is always a burning hearth at the center of his gestures, unlike the installation artist who puts his material and the arrangement of his material in a space. We would then say that the installation is literal, it needs the vanishing line of perspective as well as that of the implied meanings of the dialectical vision, or of the evidence of the narrowest symbolism (the fine art of semblance), to rediscover its meaning and its word. Because they upset differences and constantly summon up identities, sculptors can instinctively come to an understanding among themselves, we would say that they do the same job, and when they address themselves to the prestige and the powers of these techniques that surround the practice of the arts, they immediately integrate them into the very heart of the sculpted object, in this central and focal fire, in such a way that the techniques are mixed into the work, without appearing to be heavy-handed or overloaded with details. More perhaps than any other form of art, a sculpted object is and manifests, in its entirety, and even if it is so in a crude or so savage or quite unexpected way, a negotiation-attraction of differences. This is its secret, not subject to any symbolism whatsoever. The double ambiguity of the object and sculpture is due to the fact that it is at the same time a center of air and of fire, that is to say a pure explosion controlled in its forms and its spaces, and an irreducible unity, which can be immediately related to the density structure and to the non-dispersed radiations of a totem. Any sculpted object is a secret totem which refers to an identity, either hidden or obvious. The sculpture radiates from its own expansion, a fire running through the surrounding spaces, where the totem resonates with its singular intensity.

In fact, the arts today are all composite. Many of the operations of the mind and the movements of sensibility, representing and describing and ordering and suggesting and embellishing and analyzing and foreseeing and convincing and predicting for those who do not see, and simply telling, have become refined or enhanced through the centuries and spaces to produce each time works of art according to the rules and the ends of the disciplines most concerned by these different functions. What were they exercising each of these times, and in a more and more infinite manner? An extension of the differents which added up in an imperceptible way, revealing beauty as they meshed across differentiated fields and as they brought together varieties and identities without confusing them and on the contrary by illustrating each of them. Thus, the same work which had at first seemed to contain an identity (for example of a people who would like to keep to its roots) in its resemblance, in truth brought it closer to another variety of the world and changed it without distorting it. The extent of the differents, that is to say the great field of energy of the differences, is the only conceivable universal, in diversity. The so-called contemporary arts, or at least those which have escaped the literal character of the fashionable works, and which would neither try to terrify nor to divert, have become complicated and composite, in that they not only emphasize and identify and reveal the differents and thus contribute to the movement of diversities and varieties, by yet illustrating them in their singularity, but also in addition and increasingly they try to catch this very operation by which differences are added without destroying one another, and also identities vary by not wasting away. The differents do not damage/spoil variety! This is why telling stories, or tales, does not end in an art of storytelling. The work of art is the object of an infinity of these operations of the mind and of these movements of sensibilities, without saying that it contributes to arousing others, which we will learn to recognize. And the work of art ventures in this way the *magnetic connections*, and it rediscovers the dark fulgurations of the first ages of the humanities.

MEASURED RHYTHMIC PROSE FOR THE ROBBEN ROCKS THAT BOUNDED THEIR SITE, AND THE WAVES OPENED IT, AND SO WE SEE IT.

The Poem of the Infinites chants in the last verse: "Here rises finally the abode of the Spirits! ..."

And it is the immense Hall of origins, where the games of wild beer and songs are played!

The sea swells, it deposits in Valhalla its froth, which never turns into chalk. And outside, it rolls furiously to Cape Town.

And out there, the sea has cut its stabbing rocks, they howl as far as the Cape, and those who have passed through the City like shadows, remember, and they look for a long time toward the jagged rocks, old toll keepers, who have forged over the night so many and so many questions.

"No, there won't come another single Good Hope here, oho! Do not dream, the sea is mad." This is what they say.

And *The Chronicle of the Masks* then pronounces: "It is the Savannah of the first night!"

And the gods, who no longer want to be gods, receive those who will grow up as Ancestors,

and they touch their hands and their eyes, and they touch their mouths, so that they may see and make tools, and sing.

And the gods touch their heads, on both sides at the same time, so that they may listen with justice and with equilibrium to the noises of the world, and that they then hear this word which the world raises, all in seclusion and in anguish and in solitude. And you finally shout, "This is the Mountain of Magic!" where a Tree has taken root.

Those who walk behind these rocks *do not inhabit*, they have no law there, and so we see that they are not the inhabitants of the place. They dug through the stupid chalk, they teach about this space in the distance or a beetle close by, and they teach those others who have misjudged them

and who count their steps, and they gather the filings of time which no longer soars,

and they mold this debris into a ball that is a second of time passed

or that is fourteen or fifteen all at once and twenty-eight perhaps,

or that is a whole night fallen over this big stiff and red and panting noontide,

and now they jump at night, seeing that these others are going to slaughter them in their sleep,

and in the morning they dig in the chalk lime, their eyes burnt,

and again, they start teaching these others once more, who could have slaughtered them the night before,

and then they touch their heads, on both sides at the same time, so that these others will finally hear the world with balance and with equity,

and as for them they shoot this ball of time and they move and they walk and they do exercises, as if to try to break the world record for the mile, less than four minutes,

and they box with application in the vacuum, it is simply so that their too tired bodies tame and untangle this ball of time where a minute is not less than a century,

And they teach but they learn, because they learn that the infinite grows in the green death of a corridor, and that the seas rush to places of the world, which are chosen.

You shout: "It is a chosen place!" And you follow the course of the barbed wire at the top of the walls like a flame which flutters from sun to sun,

Those who walk on this Table *will really dwell there when they have left it,* having conquered the chalk and the sergeants,

Oho the sea is not complicit, wash the sea of such outrage, the seas have come running!

Robben pushes its troop of rocks to the Cape, it is a trail of suspension points,

We salute the beauty subjected to so many crimes, yesterday subjected to the *pass* and to the prohibition, and which rises here. Beauty.

Mandela Sisulu Sobukwe Kathrada Mbeki a Tree has taken root,

Raising from the shadow a light and from the light a night, and from the light a first night, Indians Zulu Black Metis White and Arab and Jews and Malagasy as much as Chicanos, and so many birds, so many of these birds, immigrants and border crossers.

NOTES IN THE COURSE OF THE TEXT, MEMORIES OF LONG TIME AGO, WORKS AND LISTS AND REPETITIONS.

In the space of a day ...: this entry into the sea also served to give landscape to a project to reprint a well-known dictionary, with some new particularities, however. The print run was very limited, at the Yvon Lambert Gallery in Paris, and the text derived through the care of Madame Jeong-A Koo, who inserted into it the subversion of the *ousss*.

The text of the language when it is formed ...: what we find for example in *The Hundred Tales* from medieval France. I have counted there many times the old word *chaudeau*, which still designates today a very particular drink in Guadeloupe, a drink served at the end of any holiday, and obtained from luxuriously prepared chocolate. But in the Middle Ages in France, it is clearly a completely different drink, with undoubtedly invigorating effects, that is brought to married couples during the wedding night, when one is assured that they have done the deed, and the bed sheet is well stained. It is above all an occasion for voyeurism and salaciousness. This meaning has been lost in Guadeloupe, the *chaudeau* is served there as much at baptisms as at weddings, when the party slows down. We have great pleasure in finding in *The Hundred Tales* the methods of making words which suit so much the creolizers of all countries, thus for *récompensation*, which I liked, which is a marriage of *récompense* and *compensation* before they were separated, and all kinds of other crazy wordings.

Timoune ...: in his *School Days*, Mr. Patrick Chamoiseau seems to lean toward *man* for the meaning of the word *moun*, his young child (the *timoune*) thinks of himself like the real *human being* of creation, and Mr. Alain Foix, on the contrary, opts for an etymology of *monde*, the young child at home is called in his work *petit monde*.

Variety...: the important notion of variety comes to me from a joke. In *Faulkner, Mississippi*, I wrote about a line in a movie about Robin Hood, a child asks Robin's Moorish companion why he is black, and the Moor replies: "Because Allah loves diversity." One of the proofreaders of the translated text proposed to render it thus: "Because Allah loves variety." (And he meant, varieties, *entertainment*.) No doubt this proofreader had been annoyed by this reference to Allah. Shocked in my turn, I soon reflected that variety is, if not diversity, at least its certain component, or its consequence. As we have said, variety is literally the unknown difference between identities, that is to say their open-ended richness. Any identity is also a variety which for a time has stopped moving. Peace to the joker proofreader.

Charged ...: a charged tree is inhabited by guardian spirits and forces, good or bad. The same goes for certain pieces of clothing.

Those who tell stories ...: at a cinema awards ceremony, and on the sidelines of all the conventions of the genre, *mom and dad*, the thanks, the tribute to the dead, a thought for the victims of disasters, another for the poor people, etc., no one will have talked about money or profit, comes a carefully worded declaration on the importance of the story tellers, saying that the tale, to tell a story, is the most universal and the most beautiful thing in the world, and that in this domain the image (cinema) surpasses the word (literature?).

The Robben Rocks ...: contribution to a photographic project on the island prison of Mr. Nelson Mandela and his comrades. (Alfredo Jaar, *The Sound of Silence*, 2006, Peter Blum Publishers) A *compact* version gives this (it is to find again, not the text, at least the emotion aroused by its pretext):

"THE ROBBEN ROCKS THAT BOUNDED THEIR SITE, AND THE WAVES OPENED IT, AND SO WE SEE IT.

The Poem of the Infinites chants in the last verse: 'Here rises finally the abode of the Spirits! ...' And it is the immense Hall of origins, where the games of wild beer and songs are played! The sea swells, it deposits in Valhalla its froth, which never turns into chalk. And outside, it rolls furiously to Cape Town. And out there, the sea has cut its stabbing rocks, they howl as far as the Cape, and those who have passed through the City like shadows, remember, and they look for a long time toward the jagged rocks, old toll keepers, who have forged over the night so many and so many questions. 'No, there won't come another single Good Hope here, oho! Do not dream, the sea is mad.' This is what they say. And *The Chronicle of the Masks* then pronounces: 'It is the Savannah of the first night!' And the gods, who no longer want to be gods, receive those who will grow up as Ancestors, and they touch their hands and their eyes, and they touch their mouths, so that they may see and make tools, and sing. And the gods touch their heads, on both sides at the same time, so that they may listen with justice and with equilibrium to the noises of the world, and that they then hear this word which the world raises, all in seclusion and in anguish and in solitude. And you finally shout, 'This is the Mountain of Magic!' where a Tree has taken root. Those who walk behind these rocks *do not inhabit*, they have no law there, and so we see that they are not the inhabitants of the place. They dug through the stupid chalk, they teach this space in the distance or a beetle close by, and they teach those others who have misjudged them and who count their steps, and they gather the filings of time which no longer soar, and they mold this debris into a ball that is a second of time passed or that is fourteen or fifteen all at once and twenty-eight perhaps, or that is a whole night fallen over this big stiff and red and panting noontide, and now they jump at night, seeing that these others are going to slaughter them in their sleep, and in the morning they dig in the chalk lime, their eyes burnt, and again, they start teaching these others again, who could have slaughtered them the night before, and then they touch their heads, on both sides at the same time, so that these others will finally hear the world with balance and with equity, and as for them they shoot this ball of time and they move and they walk and they do exercises, as if to try to break the world record for the mile, less than four minutes, and they box with application in a vacuum, it is simply so that their too tired bodies tame and untangle this ball of time where a minute is not less than a century. And they teach but they learn, because they learn that the infinite grows in the green death of a corridor, and that the seas rush to places of the world, which are chosen. You shout: 'It is a chosen place!' And you follow the course of the barbed wire at the top of the walls like a flame which flutters from sun to sun. Those who walk on this Table *will really dwell there when they have left it*, having conquered the chalk and the sergeants, Oho the sea is not complicit, wash the sea of such outrage, the seas have come running! Robben pushes its troop of rocks to the Cape, it is a trail of suspension points. We salute the beauty subjected to so many crimes, yesterday subjected to the pass and to the prohibition, and which rises here. Beauty. Mandela Sisulu Sobukwe Kathrada Mbeki a Tree has taken root.

Raising from the shadow a light and from the light a night, and from the light a first night, Indians Zulu Black Metis White and Arab and Jews and Malagasy as much as Chicanos, and so many birds, so many of these birds, immigrants and border crossers."

Border crossers or forcers...: after the overly long twists and turns of the hunt for illegal immigrants in Europe, United Kingdom and France and Spain and Italy, and the smaller mobilized principalities, one of these television channels shows in early 2006 some of these migrants brought back by force to Mali, where one of them makes an installation for local children, in the middle of the desert or in the middle of wasteland, to teach them what it is to attempt to pass through a border barricade, it is a fence planted there all in disrepair, one of those that serve to signal rather than to protect a garden, punctuated with silhouettes like flies, one would say eaten by the fence, and all tiny torn wounded, who try to climb this infinity, the camera flutters, from this surrounding sand in the face of the children to the quiet gesticulation of the demonstrator, I would have liked to have seen more closely and long enough such a work, both of art and of rigorous history, but this camera wanders, vacillates, cameras are not always equipped to catch the *magnetic trace* nor the elementary force or the connivance either. An installation which is not one, the fence hiccups in the scorching wind, this is certainly not a literal art, which for once opens up this surrounding space and which gives itself to the ephemeral and to the *reasoned disorder* of all the bloods under this sun. And the illustrator confirms calmly that, no longer for the children who already know all this but straight toward the camera, he will start again, and that he cannot come back to his village empty-handed, and that he will try again, and that he will never be afraid of dying, and that finally the barbed wire fences pricked with human meat are not invincible.

This is why the Ports, slavers or not, move us so much ...: and also the caves and the caverns and the cells and the irreparable separations and confinements, Auschwitz and the incommunicable, Gorée, Robben, the Fort of Joux, and the cave of Tjibaou, the snows of the Gulag, Saint-Pierre of Martinique and all the volcanoes of the Americas, Rapa Nui in the center of the inconceivable, Matouba in ashes, the plantation barded with canes, Carthage and the black salt, and the belly of these slave ships, the salt taxes and the red salt, and Hiroshima and Nagasaki, the smalah of Abd el-Kader, and the Great Wall so far to reach and to finish, and Socrates's cell, and the library of Timbuktu, New Orleans and its Katrinas of water since forever, pesticides plumbing the infinities of bananas, and the volcano of Empedocles, that, so they say, of Wolfgang Paalen in Mexico, yes the particular Gehennas in all these bacchanalia of misfortune, the favelas that pile up on one another all over the world, the slave trade in the fires of the Sahara and the deserts of the East, and the garrotes of Atahualpa, Circe in the dark hole of oblivion, Greenpeace in the wind of its boats of foam, and Lisbon and San Francisco and these tremors, Atlantis, Baghdad, the Styx, and for me the miserable agony of the Lézarde River. But no matter what you say, you will never get to the end of the list. In a way, a Port is a cave, with its depths and its gullies. There is no place so near or so far from you as a Port, except for perhaps a boulder or a trail of rocks in the sea, or a ghetto at the end of a snowfield, in an impassable continent, or an open-pit gold mine in Brazil. And then why do you want to force the memory of those who have forgotten, if you yourself do not have the breath to enter and walk in the cave, or the innocent goodness to mix things in the distance, we must all remember together, and the memories are shared out like a rhizome.

And some had knowledge of it, and As you already know …: and how many other quotations too well known to be really surreptitious, but in my turn I give in to the pleasure of quoting without giving a reference, with the reassuring certainty that the reader will not be taken in. Great pleasure to wander in the almost-said and the unsaid of Relation.

But no matter what you say, you will not get to the end of this list …: everyone remakes for himself the report if not the enumeration of the misfortunes with which he was in contact, of which one would not dare to say that he has been the witness, and he reimagines the misfortunes which strike afar, of which he pretends to lead the exegesis. Books in memorial persuade us that this misfortune of the people is without respite, and their accumulations lead to the dizziness of the conscience.

The languages-langages of sung orality…: these composite languages, the most often Creoles, we have said of them that they are for themselves, in the haste of their formation, their own *langage*, and that thus they had to establish new relationships with the texts they produced. The language of Montaigne is and is not the French language, this *langage* of Montaigne composes with the language and sometimes creates it, he had time to do it, in a specific way, but the Creole text, mixed up in the urgent orality of its language, and carried away in the current rush of talks and discussions, will have to invent liberating relations with it, and a distance which would allow it to escape at once from literality in this language. This is both an advantage and a lack. Profusion and severity, and constraint and freedom, in having to invent and apply *on the spot* the new laws of the relation between a text (a *langage*) and the language or languages in which or through which it is so recently registered.

Globalizations bring good and bad, globalities ...: and these globalizations proceed by complementary mechanisms in the inextricable part of the world, now that one of the unstoppable conditions of this mechanization, emerged from the obligation to have to *bring* direct benefits, is that the machine always produces the undifferentiated, the universally neutral, even if it means disguising it under the folkloric and dancing attractions of false particularities, this neutral of things and people being proposed as the only universal, that of *values*. The law of profit and the massiveness of its methods in no way allow us to calculate in time through the infinite differences. Thus, globalization will ignore the differences, and especially their realized quantity. And globality, on the contrary, is the only dimension where we can estimate both the realized quantity of all the differences in the world and the infinite relation maintained from one variety to another, from one identity to another, which come from movements of this quantity, that is to say thus, commerce and exchange, the law of which would no longer be the most eternal profit possible but the balances of give and take. Globality is not a hidden technique of the notched mechanisms and dull jolts of investment, but an art and an intuition of the moving and the global as it constitutes them itself, and in which it is given to us to live and to create. Globalism is not limited to this beautiful utopia of generality, because along the way it allows us to embolden all kinds of realizations of detail, and of those little things taken in great conceptions, and of the joys contained in their zones, which are born from each one and speak for all. Thus, it allows us to frequent our places and to invite there the places of the world, "act in your place, think with the world."

And also the caves and the caverns and the cells ... if we do not come to terms with the misfortunes of the peoples, we can bring together the landscapes, and as far as I am concerned, the capes and peninsulas which announce archipelagos, entered into my geography and which have constituted here and there a particular story in the histories of the world, Gorée at the western tip of Africa from where the Africans were thrown into the unknown and the Dubuc castle at the point of the Caravelle in Martinique where the now slaves were landed, at least a small part of them with regard to the immense landing stage and the countless trading posts and dumping sites in the Americas and the Robben Islands in front of Cape Town where Mr. Mandela fortified himself and survived for so long and which took much less time to enter our geographies and Fort de Joux near Pontarlier where Toussaint Louverture was thrown and where he died of hunger and cold and I still imagine this castle as a boat navigating the foothills of the Jura and beating with its bow the swells of the black forests, all places of imprisonment and liberation, which for me are at outposts of the seas and the oceans. Thus, not only the places that we have known but also the bursts of rocks that have marked us are intertwined in solidarity. Each of us brings one another closer to one another and in their own ways their rivers, or mountains, or canyons or forests and bushes, bays or lakes, valleys or fjords, which share geographies and which assemble the histories of the world, all the rivers where peoples burned fires for the clarity of their water, and the mountains where so many others plummeted, and the great valleys and the gullies through which cut the faint traces of the maroons, and the bush where so many maroons and rebels gathered. Bringing them together each time in a poetry or a chaos-opera, is a fertile way to dispossess oneself of these places, to better know them. The poetics of the Whole-World come from the imaginaries of our most scattered, most obstinate politics, here and everywhere, ignored and misunderstood combats and fragile gatherings and sightings so impossible to hold.

Hegel could be wrong …: it is a novel, almost two centuries old, to put in apposition the lucid and so meticulous complexity of this system of Hegel and the blindness with which he applies it to the totality of things. He lifted up beauty, it was without vision and without Relation. He knew history, he recognized it, it remained invalid, with no memory of any distant place that may be nearby.

Languages of Fragments

MEMORY IS INNUMERABLE BUT SHARED, FORGETTING IS A WEAPON WITHOUT GRACE.

Here then is the moment of illumination and explosion, and as if it were an eruption of the moon, or waters that swell without threatening, we meet here, and right here, the rock of evidence torn from so many ancient certainties, and there arises a shudder of approach and consent, it was therefore that, we were so used to rupture and denial, we did not want to think that this rock was sustaining its assembled energy on its own, and there, here is the *magnetic connection, and the trace, and the thought of the tremor,* which exercise their presence, and for all we may say, it was simple and daring to imagine that the thought of the tremor suited what quivered in the magnetic alchemy of the arts and representations, and that the thought of the trace flashed from one to the other, with a quivering divination. Here is this new space, where the crossings for millennia had been held between so many regions so little known to each other. Perspective and its techniques, and its infinities, would perhaps suggest that those who had forethought and then invented them had also had the power to push to this infinity of vision the other communities, either other or first or primitive or indigenous, and thus named, which they had encountered at the end of their drifting around the world, then these communities had been amassed to this limit and then tapered into the exploitation that they had been able to carry out, and these communities found themselves far from this line of writing which henceforth envisaged and sorted the world, indiscriminately designated and drawn as little as possible, we trade with them quite silently and we forced them to work and their land was torn down without really distinguishing between them, neither lands nor communities, and the blessed beneficiaries of these calculated profit maneuvers never had the opportunity to perceive, unless by reported accounts, these distant tools of production and profits, the extreme of perspective allowed these erasures and these infinite depths and these abysses into which anyone could be plunged. But we now know that the calculated blindness of the entrepreneurs was as fatal to themselves as to their enterprises. You cannot without risk and worry *not see* the world in which you are living and from which you also profit. The more you limit yourself to confining knowledge of it to what you call objectivity, be that of the chronicle or scientific or of varieties, which also allows you to secure and triumphantly manifest visible positions of superiority, the brilliance of *universal* colonial exhibits, and yes yes yes you have conceived both existence and being, and the more this Whole-World will impose on you the irresistible imagination of its Relation. We then pile up, alongside the infinities of perspective, so subtle and so considerate of realities, all that we have amassed from several sides of these seas, and we do not accommodate in our works backgrounds and gradations, we do not exploit chiaroscuro, we visibly and irreducibly accumulate the present onto the past, with a single square section, we break the everyday phenomena of our lives and our visions in not only the far away but especially in the whirlwind and in the spiral, where the perspective line has not yet made its way, and we give up representation for once, to always approach the inapproachable magnetic filings and the trembling realities of the Trace, it is our duty and our choice in this Whole-World, there where so many others, we happily consent to it and they willingly work alongside us, and discovering one another mutually, continue to walk their courses of writing and representation at the end of the base line of this perspective-*there*, and this one-*here* surprises then and in this way and perhaps other uses in the circularity of the universe, no longer of involuntary offensiveness but of renewed intuition, and this is revealed, all at the same time, *and that's right, yes it's because you have to put everything together, and at the same time.* The aesthetics, exploded piled up swarms, designate the totality. There, to have everything together with a single balance, and the offended histories whose sails are to be raised, and the unknown landscapes that we will suddenly see again and of which we frequent the genres, and in particular the peninsulas and the rocks, which are pathetic introductions to the islands and archipelagos but just as much to the continents, and the continents themselves which have this patience to leave the straight and triumphant ways of their old dominions to enter into the troublesome pleasures of multiplicity and sharing, and this disorder itself, which is not here the announcement of a dilution or of a partition of the self but the unassured assurance that so many definitive and systematic truths of yesterday carry gangrene into the humanities, and this or that, disturbances of diversity or praise of landscapes, do not come from religion or a belief that evaporates, and the efforts of the muscles and large organisms of the Whole-World, like a body that stands on its feet, move to spread the belief in justice and equity among peoples, and this is certainly not compassion nor, on another side, of those irreversible sworn fanaticisms, and the ruptures and fractal causes and escapades of all things in the world are added and continued, *the cry is of indecipherable woven music*, this in the last place is in any case no longer an aesthetic of the edge of the stage, so assured in everything and so effective, but of the ungovernable and all-risks encounter of our overturned aesthetics. And just as there are no patterns or themes to repeat, the horses of the Primatice or of Paolo Uccello that Mr. Alain Borer showed us in flight ("*Che cosa la prospettiva!*") or the Senufo birds which suddenly invade the space of the room of a painter from Paris, or the underground waters of the temples of the Andes which rise in floods, or the stellar interfaces of Matta, which indeed we suddenly find repeated everywhere, in the same way, the various modes of expression or figuration, realism or naturalism, and verismo, the raw and the burnt, nor the terror and the blood spilling, the abstract and the concept, rap and ragga, the tale and the lamentation, which indeed you find repeated everywhere, there is much more to it, of the sudden growth of the countries and the landscapes, of all the sides of these seas, and which will be found together, in all the blazing surroundings of all these cities and in their dark labyrinths, and then unstoppable ravages inherited from so many ancient passions, the house opposite and the street nearby and the neighboring districts and the contiguous countries which had to be destroyed, which had to be destroyed at all costs, and from the need to see together that which comes there and approaches one another, and recognizes one another, and consequently of the poetic urgency and the practical urgency raised among us, of having to fight together the oblivion which is the most perfect of all the imaginable abysses and voids, let us not allow any abyss of oblivion to bury itself in any part of the Whole-World! and at the end, finally, fragments and shatterings and radiations and propitious piles that beauty has brought about between these differences of the world, between all these differences of the world, which touch and admit and avow one another, so slow and so decisive. In my wanderings, I had brought together Chancay art from Peru and, in Mali, Bambara art, as much for what they were by themselves as for their relationships with the arts that accompanied them in their respective surroundings. We have to cross an ocean and a continent, both immense, and centuries of misunderstandings, to finally establish this relationship.

Why seek to force the memory of those who have forgotten, either by convention or inclination or calculation, or even by never knowing what was important in their History? No, we don't want that, memory cannot be controlled, it is practiced. Whoever has never known has no memory, it is true, but in this case, forgetting is not a disease, it is a total closure, like a birth infirmity. If, on the other hand, you happen to forget the condition you have made for someone, you offend them, by considering that this condition was not even worthy to be retained by you. If you forget the condition that someone made for you, you give up the peculiarity of dialogue that connects you to that someone. And as far as collective memories are concerned, the reciprocity is even closer. You cannot hate a people or a community who have stopped hating you, you cannot truly love a people or a community who still hate you, or who silently despise you. This is because, in matters of relations between communities, forgetting is a particular and unilateral way of establishing relations with others, but that memory, which is not a medication for forgetting but literally its brilliance and openness, can only be common to all. Forgetting offends, and memory, when it is shared, abolishes that offense. Each of us needs the memory of the other, because it is not a virtue of compassion or charity, but a new lucidity in a process of Relation. And if we want to share the beauty of the world, if we want to be in solidarity with its sufferings, we must learn to remember together.

At the end of the 1970s, there were enough of us, either privately or in official organizations, to raise so to speak the question of earthquakes, tsunamis, and volcanic eruptions, all natural disasters very obviously linked to one another, and to call for the necessary international preventive measures, but not one suspected the terrible radicality of what was to come, or to consider the danger of the wars over water and the lightning-quick desertifications, but not one conceived of the terror which was going to follow in this domain, or to protest also against the sanitary shortages of the majority of the countries of the world or for plans for a comprehensive resolution against extinctions by famine, but not one envisioned the destruction of populations which even today spread over Africa like relentless flights of vultures. So strong and far that the memory of the old catastrophes goes up and is maintained on its own, it will not allow to recapitulate them nor to imagine the consequences or the real fallouts from them. The memory of these calamities also seems not to cross seas and oceans, it is buried in the very places from which it originated, it is our first poetic concern. We need to recompose the archipelagic and continental fabric of our memories and to connect it in rhizomes over the entire expansion of our histories and the future of our geographies. The first desire to resist the effects of catastrophes, so deeply linked to the maneuvers of tyrannies, is a poetics before being a politics. And the feeling and the vision of the whole allow us as much to invent the details of our particular interventions, poetics does not come in hails of dreams, it is the germinated lucidity of the depths. A trembling lucidity, however. And it will not be a question of narrowing these seas and oceans where our memories are diluted, but of seeing arise on the open sea this new region of the world, into which we are all entering. Let us remember together, on all the sides of these seas! Memory is an archipelago, we are in it as islands from which the inspiring winds lead to unmoorings.

THERE HAVE NOT BEEN FOR MILLENNIA
SO MANY CROSSINGS ESTABLISHED
AND SUSTAINED BETWEEN SO MANY
REGIONS OF THE WORLD WHICH ARE
SO UNKNOWN TO ONE ANOTHER.

Really learning about the sea is quite another thing. What you need most on the oceans, and even if you do not suffer from seasickness, and even if the water barely moves around you, from those tremors which are at the birth of all things, is the privilege of bearing imbalance, in other words the ease with standing on one toe for as long as it takes. Being able to slide over water, or hover a few millimeters above its surface, or dive without losing yourself in its abysses, represents an inalienable advantage, if only to get you out of your bed noiselessly. Balance is a passion of so many movements, as the image of the thousands of wing beats of the hummingbird projects to us. And if your skin does not accommodate either sea salt or the scratches of the winds, do not follow the route of the privileged ones who unite the Capes to each other, trying to gather up unknown seas and seas hidden from all these seas, too wide for you to imagine their coasts, and in their course they do not foresee the masses of humans who for millennia have been trying to ignore or annihilate one another, from all sides of these seas. The turmoil and the immensity of all these techniques that we have moreover not ceased to praise are also like an ocean where only some keep their balance. Surfing on the dazzling screens is an additional richness, if it is to prepare your morning coffee without shocks or surprises. One of the excesses of the humanities is to know if we, that is to say, those who control such machines, will one day enter into the burning rhizomes of their circuits and their codes, hitherto prohibited. Is the virtual world a double of the real world, and would the poetics of trembling, those of the trace, vanish in the once again linear explorations of these dazzling universes? There emerge in these other partialities, a charter of the privileged, those who accede to this world and those who watch it pass by. The magnetic connections would communicate between all of them, but not the mastery of these so-called techniques, which seems to be reserved for a few. Crossings for millennia have kept these regions of our imagination separate. Those who hover in their speed and balance, and those who dive into the disequilibrium.

Decomposed, Recomposed

FRANCOPHONIE, SUSPENSION POINTS, QUESTION POINTS

1.   An effort at the same time indistinct and generous to join together, in the harsh whirlwind of the current world in fact, kinds of gathered sheaves, but flexible and binding, which would resist better the scattering of all things. A natural temptation among those who, through colonization, have nevertheless contributed to the unity-diversity of the world. And the former colonial powers share this penchant for gathering around themselves the remnants of their enterprise, especially in the maneuverable terms of culture, language, and other means of expression. In any case, the most malleable surplus to show, after the exploitations have *visibly* ceased. These gatherings appear all the more necessary that powerful blocs, themselves the result of or escaping from the colonial enterprise and history, American-Anglophone, Hispanic-American, Chinese, Indian, Brazilian, etc., have developed concurrently on the world scene. On the fringes of the real conflicts of economic interests, new forms of contact and relating are woven between cultures and communities, in a striking and unforeseeable manner, on the level of languages, ways of living, relationships with the world, which threaten perhaps to level or neutralize indiscriminately the foundations of all these cultures in contact, and consequently to swallow up isolated, fragile cultural entities or realities, likely to be assimilated in and by this enormous movement, before they could make their contribution to it. The former colonizing nations are trying to take advantage of these situations and overcome this unforeseeable element, to cast their shadow still over these fragile worlds.

But French-style colonization was also more often of a rather assimilationist character, and a Francophonie, which would be its only de facto continuation, would risk being very quickly paralyzed by this nature, even if it is underlying or imperceptible. The more practical English-speaking Commonwealth presents much more relaxed features, and a much less visible or centralized organization. In fact, the English language has perhaps dominated more the countries that it has "covered," it is much more synthetic and empiricist, it is a common place, but it has done it in a less "essentialist" way, and by respecting much more the cultures that it met there. We would say that Anglo-American is easier and less costly to adopt. (Common places: "There are difficult languages, including French." The answer: "No language is difficult for those who practice it.") The Latin American nations are today the main carriers of the Spanish language in all its diversity, and Brazil is the most important of the Lusitanian metropolises. The fate of the languages of colonization depends to a large extent on the former colonized themselves and on the way in which they will have understood their relation to languages in general. All other common places difficult to misjudge. If the unqualified domination of the United States over the world calls for the idea of an arrogant and sometimes ignorant imperial capital, France, almost alone of these former colonial powers, gives off the air of a universalizing cultural home, of the meeting of the spirit and the fine intellectual style, for those who practice or have practiced the French language, even if it means for us to decide if this involves more or less latent attempts at partial and limited domination, or if this presages a renewed cultural energy in real contact with the energy of the world.

Francophonie as an institution has been slow to understand (or to admit) that the defense of the threatened languages of the world cannot be accompanied by the sense, even implied, of a linguistic hierarchy, and that therefore France as a nation would benefit from protecting and developing the so-called regional languages which enrich its heritage, and that the whole of Francophonie itself would benefit from defending the living or dying languages which rise or fall on its territory, that likewise there are no longer any legitimate centers or peripheries, and that consequently the advantages of an absolutely centralizing language are not obvious, that moreover power does not found greatness, and that in spite of everything we must believe in the future of the small countries, and be sensitive to it. If Francophonie shakes off its phantoms, which still stammer the precepts of governing unicity, it risks in all beauty finally being part of the adventure of the world, and ceasing to be an official imposition or an eminent bias, to become an inspiration and to breathe new life.

2. We cannot claim that French literature is narrow, under the pretext that today and most often it brings to light fashions and current events. One should not exaggerate, and a literature which includes names like those of Gracq, Butor, or Le Clézio cannot be deemed without magnitude. It is true that these are the world-writers, and that the ordinary ceremonial

of literature in France tightens rather in loops, around a few places. I believe that this aspect is completely provisional. It is difficult, when one has governed the sight and the utterance of the world, which one dominated, to then find there or to accept one's place there with precision, among the others. But literature, in all countries, has always proceeded by leaps and bounds, and suddenly. It will probably be so, once again. You revel in the treasures accumulated yesterday by this French language. It will invent others. It does not dominate the world, it shares in it, at least that is what we wish for it.

3. The withdrawal into an essential language, which we consider threatened, is the reflexive recourse of those who refuse these new divisions of the world. Everyone usually prefers to believe that he speaks or writes a language dictated by a god, rather than a language which would have borrowed from everywhere, which would have been aggregated by creolization, and which would change, without losing itself or its nature. Yet it is the magnificent stake that must be risked today. Any language which, on the contrary, fixes itself on a pretended legitimacy of foundation will be swept away by the movement of the new Relation. The *receptiveness* of languages, their capacity for divination, their ability to flow in the current of exchanges and to find there their anchoring points will probably be the best guarantees of integration into the inextricability of the world. The most difficult thing then remains to overcome the economic conditioning of the language, an obligation imposed on all languages except the Anglo-American Sabir. It is better to believe in these necessities rather than in a false and angry purity of the languages we use. The normative stabilizations of languages are most often favored by periods of equilibrium in societies where they are exercised, otherwise these exasperated norms, as is the case today in the chaos-world, become restraints and handicaps.

4. The other impossible aspect of Francophonie would be a position adopted by France, with regard to the question of the integration of immigrants on its soil, and which would tend toward repressive limitation. Such a perspective, whatever the problems raised by the influx of immigrants, would be incompatible with French participation in a true gathering of an international nature, such as Francophonie would claim to be. We must also think of the real problems of integration on the basis of this international order (or indeed disorder), and not only by confining ourselves to the immediate profits that we could make on a local level. After having admitted generally all the immigrants, because it had need of them and for this reason alone, France could not decide unilaterally, today, on a "selective" immigration and an integration based on "value," without

taking into account the situation in the world and its place in this world. The evolution of societies, which is a ferment, never proceeds by careful and selective decantations. The integration of the immigrants could be done in harmony only on the basis of a politics of Relation, which has yet to be invented, and of which, moreover, all participants in Francophonie should be the stakeholders.*

From *Les Inrockuptibles*, March 2006.

IMAGES OF EXISTENCE, PLACES OF THE IMAGINARY.

Thank you for having me here and for initiating what I hope will be a fruitful exchange. My point of departure will be what I call a "naive thought," and which it is, as opposed to what would be a "scientific thought," and I will begin with a modest but resolute praise of this "naive thought." Of course, this can lead to anthropomorphisms, when it ingenuously tries to relate the real to the very model of man taken in his generality. And there is another form of naive thought which seems interesting to me, and which I will call a "geomorphism," when it tries, by a completely opposite movement, to bring back the constituents of the humanities taken in their generality to a poetic geography and geology which surpass them by integrating them. So, these two movements, anthropomorphism or geomorphism, are recognized to be opposite in their directions, but they correspond perhaps in a deep way to some much more imperceptible dimension, which is that the human species tends to make equivalent and interdependent the oscillations of its being and the movements of the world. This has always been the ambition of the poets. We know that from the moment Plato decreed the laws of the City, and that he banished the poets from it, it was in the name of reason which will later be called pure, or which will later give birth to scientific thought, but that in our opinion it was above all because of the fear he felt in front of the frightening capacity of poets to let themselves be taken into the obscurities of myth and the legends of the beginnings. Naive thought, in particular in its geomorphism, is a public deformation of this inclination of poets, since their banishment far from reason and from the City, toward a specific poetic knowledge. Plato had confined them to the expression of feelings, joy, pain, love, melancholy, hatred, filial piety, rural pleasures, this is lyrical poetry, the better to forbid them any possibility of entering knowledge by means other than those of the science that Aristotle will define later. And poetic knowledge, to return to Plato's fears, is indeed knowledge from the depths. Aimé Césaire, in a text published in the review *Tropiques* (Martinique, 1945), recapitulates this question, and the text is titled very precisely "Poetry and Knowledge." It appears, in the history of Western cultures, that there was there something that we had to try to reach, and that the means of logic and science, the foundations of these cultures, were not enough on their own for us truly to reach it.

In one of his *Five Great Odes*, "The Muse which is Grace," Paul Claudel, if only in the name of Catholic unanimity alone, supports this renunciation of a simply decorative function of poetry, "And the poet replies: 'I am not a poet ...'" I am not a poet as Plato defined it, "and I am not here to make you laugh or cry," I am a poet who intends to go to the bottom of this abyss, and who intends to carry out in full the principles and the germinations of another knowledge. All this is at the source of naive thought and this thought, which is not the thought of poetry, which is not the search for depths, but which is already the renunciation of frameworks, the joyous refutation of dictates, conceives, as originary, the rejection of any absolute truth and the rejection of any system of thought. It is therefore from the point of view of this naive thought that I would like to question the notions that Western philosophies have consecrated under the names of "existence" and "being," in that existence appears there as an absolute, an unattainable, as a transcendence or a sublimity, which are not characteristics there since neither the absolute nor transcendence are characterized, but can be designated as attributes of existence. But again, could existence be able to accommodate attributes? And in so far as being appears there as the relative, if one can say, one can walk in being, it includes territories, no, lands, it admits vastness, and that if it is difficult to speak of the qualities of existence, it is possible to do so for being, but these qualities of being are not qualities of existence, they are variables.

This dimension of existence governs Western philosophies, and the mystical thoughts of Islam for example, where it occurred that this thought of existence, and existence itself have been considered as a scandal, an interesting proposition if we put it in apposition to the Heideggerian philosophy, and as for us, and today, we discern with difficulty but clearly the outline of a thought of the border. If by the principle of geomorphism we "geographize" being—let us say it this way—the notion of the border immediately emerges. The border is what connects two states of being, as in the real world the border separates two states or two communities of the world. This notion of the border has insidiously inclined the intellectual activities of humanities toward organization into a system. The system (systematic thought and the system of thought) has two borders in sight, the one on which it leans and the one toward which it tends, the system does not take care of any possible right-hand borders, or left-hand borders, in other words the system goes in a single direction and defines a linear aim. The concept of border thus conceived is irremediable, because it poses at the same time what is the same and what is the other, promised separately, in a radical and impassable way, and without any road that crosses or meanders. We do not cross these borders by wandering on the edges. Under these conditions, Western thought has evolved, in the linear fashion I have indicated, toward conceptions which define the object to be achieved as sufficient for itself, in full objectivity, always situated on this line between two borders, one of which is irremediable in the past, the other unattainable in the future. The notion of border thus understood is obsolete, and after all these advances in thought, the moment comes when the border can no longer be considered as watertight, and where the idea grows that it no longer has any reason for being as such. Being is not a territory marked out by borders, but an inexplicable structure, in revolution on itself. The border is no longer one of the possible facts of being, but in our world a flight of passages, and of in-betweens, which are easy or difficult to cross, but which will henceforth be crossed in every way.

In other words, the border, which had no relation to existence (in traditional conditions, existence is an absolute, there is no *border-existence* of existence), has emerged from the rank of being to enter into the order of existence, precisely because it has ceased to be an impossibility and become a passage, and that existence, in our poetics, has ceased to be an absolute for becoming a Relation. There are borders, not certainly of existence but in existence, which we will have to approach. The effort of contemporary thought, through manifestations that we could bring together side by side, the sciences of chaos, the fractal sciences of psychoanalysis, the aesthetic derivatives of the inextricable things of the world, and the growing sciences of the environment (that is to say of the necessary relation between the biological beings and the organic beings and finally the geophysical phenomena), the explorations of the poetic fields and whether they can retain the speed, the fulguration and also the thickness and the measure of time, the experiments of the voice and of orality and if they can endure like writings, the learning of rhythms and if there are any that are fundamental or ephemeral enough to reconstruct traces, the tormented attempts of democracy and if it can really be direct, all this aims to establish that in the depths of existence, or Relation, are allowed borders, passages, the difficulty of our poetics being to know first how to find again these passages and then to know how to navigate them. The function of the border, this mediation between reflection and operation, is to fade away into the geopolitics of existence, the variables of being are multiplied and are relayed to infinity, and to emerge vividly in a geopolitics of existence, the absolute of existence has entered Relation. We need this border and its metamorphoses, to exercise our ease in moving from one same to this other. And poetics, whatever their fields of application may be, are thus concrete practices.

These affirmations are so many heresies, I believe so, but according to which credo? The inextricable nature of the humanities in the world allows us these leaps. We see there that being is perpetually expanding, in the exact image of what the scientists say about the universe, that it is continuously expanding. They also say that we will come, that is to say the universe, to an ultimate phase, a stasis, where it will stop expanding, it would be like a final border, *everything* will remain in a prodigious balance, then perhaps this whole will flow back, and will undertake to shrink, until it comes back, by such a tiny unimaginable contraction, to the primordial molecule disintegrated by the big bang. It is too formidable a prospect, and it is certainly not easy for the mind, at the very least, to calculate this reduction, in billions and billions of years, to the first molecule. Being grows larger, and existence remains, but in the hypothesis of a shrinking of the universe, both will follow the same course of a tragic diminution. Even if the hypothesis is false, or inadmissible, the mere possibility of its evocation makes the exercise of thought dramatic. Closing our eyes, like Kant, we can accept or at least confront the prospect of the disappearance of the humanities, not that of the annihilation of existence and of being. Neither essence nor the accident perish. From the point of view of naive thought.

It seems that it is this unacknowledged fear, not only of an annihilation of the humanities but also of a dilution of their essence, which has led a large part of the cultures of men, out of the desire for eternity, to trace the passage of existence to oneself, that is to say to an identical, and from this identical to identity. And in response, it is in identity that is conceived the identical, that is conceived the self, and that is conceived existence, which in its formulation has never been geomorphic but anthropomorphic. Reflecting on this question of identity, I who am of a community whose identity has always been denied, not only as a reality but as a principle—which would pose a difficult problem for anyone who would like to analyze a Martinican or an Antillean—I find that one of the shortcomings of colonized societies was to adopt, without critical reflection, the principles of identity of their colonizers. And especially in the "composite" countries, that is to say those born of history. These are societies which have not created, invented, called for, or developed a Genesis. Their origin does not go back to a mythical time—we come back to Plato and to the passion of poets for myths and original depths—but to a crossing or a reversal of history, invasions, colonizations, immigrations, mixing. The genesis of our societies and our Creole cultures is not an original paradise, it is the belly of the slave ship, which in this case was the only absolute. Poetics then and in general pour out a cry from the depths, the echo of myth, to the word of Relation, the rhizome where existence and being are equivalent. Our colonized societies, however, adopt without any critical revision the closed dimension of the identity that the various colonizers have indicated to us. Most of the old anti-colonialist struggles in the world have been waged according to these approaches of an absolute identity, and have been catastrophic, in their consequences, their extended effects, their sectarianism, national egoisms, the non-relation to the other. The obsessive and stubborn idea that identity, like existence, is an absolute, an in-itself that runs on this line of which I have spoken, with these ancient borders ahead and behind.

(Let us recompose on our charts, in as few clear figures as possible, what we have. The composite societies, born from history and its encounters, readily adopt myths of origin from elsewhere. There will follow, in these new societies, a remarkable mixture and creolization of these Geneses, which are at their origins uncompromising. What every Genesis authorizes, in an atavistic society, is an absolute legitimacy guaranteed on a territory by this creation of the world, followed by a process of filiation, itself protected by systems of legitimacy. The tables of filiation are not so close to each other, so the line of ancestors in sub-Saharan Africa is not exclusive, a foreigner can enter it. The Geneses are not all absolute, thus the Amerindian gods were wrong three or four times before succeeding in the creation of the world and the humanities; the ferment of relativism and of doubt, let us say of trembling, is at the source of this creation. A god that doubts and makes mistakes is of great help to our human uncertainties. And the legitimacy of filiation is, moreover, and from the beginning threatened, in these Amerindian theologies, there is in fact an obscure and unknown period which extends its abyss between the creation of the first man and the beginnings of human history. In all possible ways, the truth does not seem transcendental. Composite societies also generate, little by little, the *thoughts* of their creation, which we could gather under the name of digeneses, nourished by the certainties of the human sciences, and these are as many attempts at syntheses based on all the sustainable historical convergences. The conception of unique root identity, which had prevailed in absolute terms in atavistic cultures, is replaced with some difficulty by that of rhizome-identity or relation-identity.) The obsession with a transcendent in-itself is gradually fading.

The question of identity is a matter of poetics, insofar as poetics have always claimed to have knowledge from the depths, essentially through the myths of origins. It also is a matter of politics, insofar as we are witnessing the metamorphosis of the absolute of existence into the principle of Relation, existence is Relation, and thus existence and being are connected in a new way. I would say that existence, which knows itself by intuition, founds the image, whereas being, which knows itself by the imaginary, establishes places. The image is the very sign of the intelligibility of Relation, which relays and connects and relates the elements of the Whole-World, which today includes all of them. In other words, Relation is the realized quantity of all the differences of the world, and is opposed to the universal which was the reference to the realizable quality of an absolute of the world. Relation allows us the passage, the ford, between all the differents of the world, whereas the universal, only yesterday, tried to abstract these differents into a truth which would have been connected to the absolute truth of existence. The place is that which in Relation, in the realized quantity of the differences in the world, is unavoidable, that is to say that through the place we see that Relation is never a dilution of the particular, a mishmash in which everything is confused and dissolves. Relation is the realized quantity of all the places in the world. We must, however, perhaps give up the idea that we will be able, by the intuition of being or by the imagination of being, by the invention of the image or by the foundation of the place, rediscover appearances of absolute truth, on a new line which would have found its point of view and its focal point. Places are founded on the inextricable part of the world, and the world is inextricable in its places. In this inextricable nature, the qualities of existence as being and of being as existence, which are no longer just variables, are themselves inextricable, opacity, the trace, the tremor.

Opacity is not only the obscure, opacity represents what a place affixes to another place as the freedom of its relation. I claim for all and for everyone the right to opacity, an embarrassing prospect perhaps for an analyst. The alleged transparency of the truth has led us away from conceiving that the links in the inextricable are not paralyzing. The thought of the tremor characterizes the approach of this inextricable world. Let us repeat that the tremor is not fear, neither fear nor hesitation, is not uncertainty erected in fantasy, but the deliberate vocation of renouncing long systematic views, to equational development, to the linear principle, as the physicists of the sciences of chaos might have said. The tremor thus plunges us into the intuition of the depths, and that there is something, both in geomorphism and in anthropomorphism, which makes all kinds of tact and contact possible, and which allows us to drift away, to deviate, in this inextricability and this compositeness of the world. Also, the old intuition of the depths responds sufficiently to the present forecast and to the reading of Relation, poetic thought, cutting through the lyricisms of convention, has passed from these depths to this Relation. The trace, however, is that by which, on which, in which the tremor advances. It resists the search for transparency (and can we say, analysis?) but it approaches the magnetic connections. Its fragility is what makes its resistance, and its transience guarantees its duration. It runs through our accumulations, our assonances, our repetitions, our circularities. The trace does not allow cunning economies of expression, nor does it allow literal replicas of our realities, duplicates without openness or invention.

(Let us recompose again. In composite countries, and for example for the Creole cultures of the Americas, advances have been made in traces. The essential of the population arrived there naked, that is to say after having been stripped of the artefacts of its original culture, its languages, its gods, its everyday objects, its customs, its tools, and it was necessary to recompose by traces, "in the desolate savannas of memory," what remained to them of the old atavistic cultures, to recognize it and elect it in exultation, and to blend it by creolization with the other cultural elements intervening in this composite. Jazz from the South of the United States, like the musical forms of the Caribbean and Brazil, first consisted of a return to the African trace, tuned to instruments from Europe, and the Creole languages of the Caribbean have also proceeded by traces to constitute their corpus, lexical and syntactic. The thought of the trace is the most sensitive of all to the magnetic connections which form the grammar of the Whole-World. And to the extent that traditional atavistic cultures, in the West or in Africa and Asia, tend today more and more toward the composite, the recourse to creation by the trace, and by the traces, which is distinguished from system-based thought, progresses and refines itself.) Having thus made the thing more complex, as Mr. Jacques Coursil would have said, we can summarize it with a dash of obscurity. Image of poetry, places of politics. But intuition could equally well relate to the political, and if in its turn the imagination runs toward Relation, it is from the depths that poetry reveals.*

Le Cercle freudien et Espace analytique, May 2005.

THE SLAVE TRADE, SLAVERY, ABOLITIONS: ALL THE DAYS OF MAY ARE POSSIBLE, AND ALL MEMORIES CONTRIBUTE.

This first commemoration in France of the historical fact of the Slave Trade, of slavery, and of their abolitions, is remarkable in that it brings together in the same event the desire for memory of the descendants of those who suffered these events and the will to memory of the descendants of those who organized them in part. In our globalized world, we too often and *unknowingly* suffer the direct consequences of the histories that we have been able to share, impose, or endure: resentment, and fear, sometimes crippling hatred, and on the other hand arrogance and impure contempt, or latent or virulent racism, all reactions born from the same ignorance of what happened, and whose revelation is often traumatic. Let us affirm that this is not a question of a requirement of historical responsibility to be recognized and assumed by anyone, that flagellation and requests for repentance seem derisory to us, but of this mutual ignorance precisely, which we really have to hunt down and address. As for the West Indian or African communities, they can very well celebrate for themselves and by themselves the victims they had to deplore in history, and consequently choose the dates which seem appropriate to them, they will do so without doubt independently. This summarizes the specific, and new and irreplaceable character of May 10, as the date proposed by the *Committee for the Memory of Slavery* and chosen by the president of the French Republic, it is the affirmed and conscious sharing of these same histories, those of the formerly expanding countries and those of the formerly colonized countries, histories long rejected from both sides of the same collective ignorance. This exchange renewed on May 10 will also promote the difficult knowledge of our world, and will undoubtedly help us understand and combat modern forms, obvious or not, of a slavery all the more devastating as it is lost from view in the upheavals of our chaos-world. Children, women, isolated nations, displaced people, immigrant communities, and how many victims that *we do not see*. The date does not matter much, May 22, May 23, May 27, our histories diverge and converge, our dates meet, our memories reinforce one another. May 10 will perhaps be their focal point, another gathering agreed upon in the diversities of spaces and times, of the places and dates of the world. It will be to France's great credit to have wanted such an event, the first government no doubt to propose it and put it into action. There are slavery museums, and one of them is under construction in Virginia in the United States, Mr. Chien Chung Pei is responsible with others for its architectural realization. It will be the U.S. National Slavery Museum (with the slogan "We are one people"). And many other organizations in Brazil and in Africa, including the Gorée Museum, the place which was the main embarkation center for Africans being trafficked to the New World, off the coast of Dakar, and whose importance and high symbolic and emotional value must be emphasized. Other communities, all along the coasts of West Africa, memorialize the slavery of their ancestors, and on this occasion sing about the sea, this Atlantic Ocean, a true accomplice of the Slave Trade, and indelibly marked by this path of suffering. We do not know if the same applies to the memory of the East African Slave Trade, to the east, to the Horn of Africa and the Arabian Peninsula, and to the west for the memory of the Trans-Saharan Slave Trade, to the north of Timbuktu.

The design of the National Center for the Memory of Slavery will be proposed by a planning committee. The Center will undoubtedly include a multidisciplinary research department, an archival nucleus to which the archives departments of public and private establishments will contribute, along with a section to decipher, read, and arrange these documents, a section for the study of the possible repercussions of this knowledge on educational programs, a large research module on forms of contemporary slavery, editorial activities, studies, work relating to art and literature, periodicals or anthologies, cultural meetings and exchanges, and finally a Memorial, to which I hope all the forces of all the contemporary arts will contribute, on all continents and in all known archipelagos. These initial approaches and proposals may be reviewed, restricted, or supplemented, first by the work of the committee itself, then during various study and discussion meetings. This outline foreshadows what would be the essential functions of such a National Center: to collect scattered knowledge, to study what in any case could not be considered nor presented as a simple series of elementary evidences, to keep alive and united the memory of all, to enrich the Relation between the communities of the world, illustrate, transmit, share. There could be no question of undertaking systematic critiques of what exists on the matter (school programs and the activities of associations and public or private organizations, etc.), but of attempting fruitful syntheses, the opening up of the memory of the Slave Trade and of slavery, and of their abolitions, cannot support unilateral and sectarian positions. On both sides of the seas and the sands where the Slave Trade traced and where these forms of slavery grew, any shared memory is the guarantor that we will strive to overturn the abysses.

Recognizing slavery as a crime against humanity, and enshrining it in law, is no more exceptional than condemning war criminals for the same reasons. The difference is in the time elapsed between the crime and its conviction, but we know that on the subject, as opinion has decided, there is no statute of limitations. The historical studies of these periods of the Slave Trade and of slavery, as for any period analyzed, are not neutral and sanitized, the consequences of these times still resound, historians could not claim the serenity or the tranquility of the laboratory to carry out successfully their work. The proclamation of a law and the study of a societal fact in turn form part of history, enter into history, and the historian takes risks just like the legislator. He cannot therefore study history as an inert matter, available in everything and perhaps malleable. As if, failing to command history, he reserved the right to decide its meaning for himself. The conviction of those who perpetrated these crimes does not mean that their descendants should be held responsible. The humanities are done with this idea of collective and perpetual responsibilities. And likewise, the thought of reparations is politically and morally impractical and unjusti-fiable. The main exception to be considered in this matter is the reform due to the African continent, whose underdevelopment was savagely hollowed out and then maintained by the Slave Trades and colonizations. This global and structural repair, the nations of the rich regions would be honored and greatened by making it happen, but it is undoubtedly a hollow vow. It would not be a question of alms or compassion, but of an urgent measure of international public utility. Our world needs a liberated Africa, which would finally devote its resources first to its communities.

Opera

THE CLOSED BELLY OF THIS SHIP, THE
DOMINATED PEOPLES, THE PEOPLES
WITH NO RESOURCES, AND PERHAPS
THE SIDES OF OUR CAVES TO COME
WILL BE SPARKLING BLINDING VOIDS
WALLS OF GLASS AND OF SO MUCH
NOTHINGNESS WITHOUT BREATH
OR ECHO.

This feeling of a brutal and so close mutation, the Caribbean Sea blows and swells with madrepores, and the little waters and the seas buried in the great Pacific Ocean rise, all this piling up and everywhere the cadences and hideousness and indifference to common sense, the streaking violence, the insult, and even *which make art*, which appear so liberating, which seem to promise the passage to another thing, to what, in any case those who suffer the impossibility of beauty, the call and the renunciation of beauty, it is all that, simply the terrifying weight of what we know can no longer reach for beauty and we stammer this helplessness, and rather we shout it in all kinds of excesses from which we make art, no longer listen to the song of the world, the world is screaming all around, and the trace is overcome and the connection dried up, because we have all failed to practice this *magnetic connection*, with not only our surroundings and the species that inhabit them (this, we can, we have, found its secret, if it is still possible), but also with other humanities, fixed or wandering (instead of enveloping them, as we do, with a moral blanket), so that all this noise that we unleash comes from the regret at no longer going toward beauty, we pile the lightning onto the crash so as not to give ourselves time to perceive the different parts of the world, which would indicate beauty, we want to overwhelm all that exists under the indistinct thunder of this thick exacerbation, this is what it is and what it will be, *the cry opens a noisy absence* and a renunciation of all kinds of difficult quests for agreements, we cut out noise so as not to have to listen to one another, we refuse the differences of the world, and the very idea that there could be difference, we recompose a huge indistinct savage *Identical*, and which means *undifferentiated*, but meanwhile, and without our having sought it, our bacchanals and our tumults have overturned languages, less than ever they *recite* and push their ruse from a beginning to an end, and here they are, these languages, crushing islands of words that arise insoluble in the enormous flood that summoned them, and the spoken-written languages become sung-oral languages and in these languages the *langages* multiply, so that this violent machine to manufacture the undifferentiated has also conceived at the same time what will fail it in so many fertile bursts, and it is the *langages* which will save the languages, at least those which will have lasted until then, and it will be these *langages* which will cherish the memories of the disappeared languages, and which will awaken among us the traces of the murdered languages, and which will weave the maze, fertile with the multiplicity of languages, then the closed seas and the seas concentrated on themselves, the Mediterranean or the Black Sea or the Sea of Marmara, will immediately bring closer together the mouths of their long rivers and the limits of their fresh and salty waters.

No place in the world can accommodate itself to the slightest forgetting of a crime, of the slightest shadow cast. We ask that the unspoken parts of our histories be conjured, so that we enter, all together and free, into the Whole-World. Together again, let us name the Slave Trade and slavery perpetrated in the Americas, a crime against humanity. Soyinka Chamoiseau Glissant March 1998.

Against all desire for a sly and calculated oblivion on the part of those who consider themselves to be the upholders of the colonial heritage, against also any tormented and angry desire for oblivion, of those who have long oscillated between the shame of the experience undergone and the pride of history reassumed. May the memories of a shame suffered yesterday not incline you to despise those who in turn relive your former lot. And that the old desire for oblivion does not turn into what it carried in the first place, an infirm rancor. Again the feeling of this brutal and so close reversal, not of a final nothingness but of a dereliction which does not stop any more, the seas in the form of a secret lake do not generate their propitious borders, another immigrant pushed back from the coasts of Spain peacefully declared that even if the whole sea around were planted with electrified wire barriers he would set off again on this cold sea, with anything, a tub, a trunk of a palm tree, an inflatable, he just had to send money to his family, what man in the world would not understand that, and the camera by chance filmed him from below, he stands like a statue, that is to say a totem, valid for all. This quality of the sculpted object retains us, in all the natural catalog of works of art. And so, that it is in Chancay art in Peru and in Bambara art in Africa, and mainly, and in any case most openly, that the most ordinary works of pottery, intended for the most common use, get just as close to the complex nature of any sculpted object, that is the totem, be it accepted or hidden. The experts think that Chancay art is not as advanced as the arts that surround it, it would be less sure of itself, less mindful, the line less firm, the representation more unpolished, and I don't think that they are so judgmental as regards Bambara art in Africa, but I see that these two arts practice in the same way, they have distanced themselves from the other force that is explored in the world of the so-called primitive or first or other arts, the flamboyant totemic fixity, so they illustrate primarily *the thought of the tremor*, the Chancay by this line that might have been called uncertain, by this apparent naivety in form and by these too quick and badly enlarged volumes, the Bambara by this profusion of carvings, by these infinite inlays which also bring us back to the prophetic dust of the trembling truths, these two arts stretch space and unburden it of its heaviness, they lighten also the weight of the world, and it is as if they create clearings in the bushiness of life without damaging it, or as if they were really arts of the sands, and of lighter higher ground, where the air thins and clarifies, and if they do not show an equal obstinacy in the stretching and widening and the slenderness of all things, the Bambara sculpted objects go infinitely farther, at least you recognize them on a first look, the one and the other art, in their respective surroundings, for these colors that they spread like transparent veils, these pale or burnt ochers, these scattered but insistent sandblasts, which weave a different kind of weariness, and which immediately appear as the manifestation right-here of a distant knowledge of that very thing which existence imposes so ardently or intensely, and very close by. Fragile arts indeed, and non-literal expressions of the suspense of the world, and light breaths in the heavy panting of the cave. The same differently, on continents so huge, so far apart from one another, but we see them together. To be a maroon is to take the crossroads of thought, to follow in the traces, to crisscross in all the detours. The prophetic vision of the past is continued in another vision, brought closer or simultaneous, of the infinites. We pass from the transparencies and opacities of the Bambara countries and the Dogon countries to the transparencies and opacities widespread on all the mountain ranges and peaks of the Andes countries, and just as quickly in the other direction, Relation runs between everything and everything, then we ask ourselves what is this we, what is this we that jumps out in so many pitfalls of thought, in so many unforeseeable circumstances in the world, in so many common-places, that you suddenly discover.

From all the sides of these seas, what resurfaces and appears as the highest novelty, in its very resurgence, is this tremor which traverses the traces and which assembles the obscurities, and we see for the first time that it is a cinema, the speeded up or the slow motion of the coasts and the deep plains and the gullies and the crests indicate to us Relation, and we are astonished that the art of cinema loses so much of space and time on its way, lingering on so many wonderfully told stories, devoting so many inventions to duplicating the world without our being able to believe that we recognize it there, and then passing far alongside the shivering and trembling, as if the cameras had on sunglasses, and also the camera holders, devices that facilitate vision and obscure the view, and we have to repeat what we have said and proposed on the inextricable. On the one hand, racial and community clashes do not seem to have to be slowed down or resolved in the world, on the contrary, it seems that the announcements made or the effects of announcements in the organs of the press contribute to reinforce what we can only call *determining gaps* (but here with totally negative effects) between the various human groups. The main "reasons" for these confrontations certainly appear to be of an economic nature, it is almost always a question of exploiting a collectivity, but another dimension is added to it, like a mystery of the relationship between diverse human-ities, an inexplicable state of intolerance and sectarianism, of which we have no idea how to solve the enigma. There are also these spectacular and unstoppable flows of immigrants from the poor countries of the Earth and toward the rich countries, their flow and their permanence help to accredit the opinion that there truly exist humanities and sub-humanities. There are no longer any slave ships, nor the flashy exhibitions of native habitats and lifestyles, nor the first ethnographic films or movies à la Tarzan, but tunnels under the borders, and dams, electric fences, boat people of all categories, walls of hundreds of kilometers, sad and often condescending commentaries. The richest countries, which had themselves organized the immigration of the poorest and least qualified individuals on their own territories, when these said countries needed it for their most disparaged and least paid tasks, and nevertheless essential to their construction or their reconstruction, now only want to accept *skilled immigrants*, as in the days of Plantation slavery there were field negroes (who were driven to exhaustion in the cane or cotton fields) and skilled negroes (who worked in the houses of the masters or who were trained in small local trades, cooks, coachmen, shoemakers, music players, etc.). But one could not conceive and build in this way a society out of carefully crafted adjustments, such a society would have been artificial in nature, close to the disquieting pictures of science-fiction novels, it would have had neither the inspiration nor the vivacity of a country existing in the world and conceiving and understanding and approaching the problems of the world. For a country like France, for example, a systematic and predetermined policy of limitative repression of immigration would be incompatible with the desire or the pretension to participate in a real gathering of an international nature, such as Francophonie would claim to be, we should really think about the problems of immigration and also of the integration of populations on French soil from this unavoidable international dimension, and not by thinking only of the immediate profits to be made by setting up a local plan. The reception and, if it happens, the integration of immigrants could only be "successful" on the basis of a *politics of Relation*, which has yet to be invented, and of which, moreover, *all the participants in Francophonie should be the tenants*. But we also know that most poor countries have no way of protecting their borders against immigration of another kind but also savage, that of the investors who exploit their resources for revenues that will immediately go elsewhere, nor afterwards in bringing back to their borders those undesirables they no longer want. The situation seems inextricable, unless we consider the gradual but final extermination of all *field immigrants*, or the parking of all these desolate countries behind barbed wires of concentration, and the mutual extinction of all the known racial and identitary antagonists, as solutions. The humanities of today have, however, the patience to invent, on the fringes of the political and social efforts that must be implemented, and that one must not stop implementing, and they would also have the foresight to follow the poetics of togetherness that direct our general politics. "The economic rebalancing of the world is an absolute necessity, and we cannot cease to consider it, even if we see most often that it is a matter of a promise that is not followed up in fact. In particular, the reform due to the African continent, whose underdevelopment has been savagely imposed then maintained by the Slave Trades and then by the colonizations, would have nothing to do with alms or compassion, but with an urgent measure of international public utility. Our world needs a liberated Africa, which would finally use its resources primarily for its communities." The Africas will defend themselves, as well as all those peoples maintained in the enclaves of subjection, but they need the unanimous protestations of all the humanities. Also, the identitarian internecine massacres will not end, so long as these same humanities will not accept to consider the identity of each one, individual or group, as inalienable and variable, in its relation to the other. *I can change in exchanging with the other, without, however, losing myself or changing my nature.* Hammering these repetitions is to openly back the resuscitation of the borders. The world is inextricable, but we learn more and more to live and think this inextricability.

In the chaos-opera of this world, as Mr. Bernard Lubat might have said, the cities carry and support. The modern cities, resulting from a mutation or created from nothing, we will not see they are destined for destruction, but in any case, that they have been built or built up, contrary to the traditional cities set in contrast and continuity with the surrounding countryside, with little thought for this connection or at least in the pleasure of the rupture. Every traditional city envisages the countryside that surrounds it, it observes it from high up on its walls, or protects itself from it by a maze of suburbs and outskirts, which are in transition. It is as if the city built itself from a flow of blood or of energetic liquid that came from the countryside and that coagulates little by little. The city, which established itself little by little, was this coagulation of that which bled from the countryside. All that, in the modern cities, is cut off, no longer by the walls or the suburbs, that would be rather elements of relation, but in the absolute. Cities of rupture, and not even of renewal, but of a blank slate. Many of these cities, in China so they say, in zones of industrial and financial overdevelopment, and extremely sophisticated, are built up on the edges of swamps that they have not had the time to fill. They have no system of venules with their surroundings. They do not contain unnecessary, non-functional parts, pushed there by chance and useless happiness. They are city-islands, urban islands without visible division. They don't know anything about what's going on elsewhere. Ignorant cities, their energy replaces their knowledge and, being sufficient for themselves, by whatever principle of domination they benefit from, they have a great advantage in ignoring everything of what surrounds them. These are cities that can do without the world, I mean, the idea of the world and the passion of the world. Their absolute autonomy is reflected in the daring they show to rise up, but since they obviously do not maintain any continuity with a past or with a surrounding space, one wonders if these are the cities that will remain, which will endure. This question of time in the city, of time of the city, is also raised brutally. These cities are consuming their time in a lightning way. They change quarters like we change our clothes. But does a city have the function of enduring? Maybe not. The modern city is perhaps an ephemeral form, and then started again elsewhere at the same time and then repeated in the same place a little later, like the settlements of nomadic peoples. But rather than this pure nomadism, it is a city in constant and total metamorphosis, while the traditional towns knew a very slow metamorphosis, and took their time to evolve. Still today, it is possible for you to visit past times. In the modern cities, you cannot really visit anything but the present, you don't encounter either the past or the future. For these are cities that are overturned from top to bottom and without anyone being able to explain why nor how nor in which directions. Would their impressive beauty, often more visible from afar, in a panorama or from above, than close up or from the inside, be made first from this tragic renouncement of beauty, that we have already claimed for current sensibilities, that is to say this renouncement of difference, *that these cities accumulate so as to no longer see them?* And the enormous undifferentiated aspect of their tumult, does it aim to uproot that, this other aspiration to agreed differences, that is to say to the differences that meet up and accord themselves, and to make its coming impossible? These tumults most often do not arise from chaos but border on nothingness. The eternal *presence* that results from such a tension and that at the same time creates it, engenders its own cries that are so many phantasms and their destructions, but never a means of reconnecting with their surroundings, with that which we would call their countryside. From the sole point of view of our aesthetics and of the literatures that envisage us, the relation of a "rural" literature to an "urban" literature is, however, that which has most marked literary expression in the second half of the twentieth century, beginning principally with William Faulkner (Literature of the Plantation). But we could go back to Tolstoy, to *War and Peace*, which stages the incessant back and forth of the Russian aristocracy, those who could live in both places, from Saint Petersburg or from Moscow to the countryside, and not only a book about war and peace but also a song of the city and the countryside, and their relationships. One of the essential arguments of the book is moreover the capture and the occupation of Moscow, for the first time cut from its countryside, and its liberation by it. The perseverance of this relationship generates a poetry of continuity, of duration. It is when Faulkner violently pushes back the city (which for this southerner is first and foremost that of the Yankees), and when Dos Passos completely ignores the countryside, that the poetics in their turn differ powerfully. But if Faulkner recomposes a duration, which in the image of his poetic intention we can qualify as *differed duration*, Dos Passos practices a literature of breaking and fracture, of mere *presence*, and of rupture, which is that of the modern city itself. Faulknerian violence is not of the countryside but of the Plantation, a real walled city, a place of the precipitation of differences, of their tragic conflicts, and of their creolization, all the more frenzied because it is absolutely rejected there. Cities carry and support, they destroy and are perhaps doomed to be destroyed, but the rupture in Dos Passos is perhaps an overly literal expression of it to be able to signify it, and the Faulknerian difference comes far closer to the secret flows of these poetics (for example, by *the Domain, the Hamlet, the Town*). Beyond or below the enormous banalizations of contemporary creations, it is in any case one of the hidden stakes of the aesthetics that interest us.

Countryside is disappearing all over the world, as technicities gain ground, one would thus say that the countrysides are hindered by underdevelopment, folklores, and inaction, and when and where the countrysides resist they no longer have presence in relation to the cities. There is no known architecture that endures still, even if in the rich countries the citizens will buy up and restore country dwellings, but the architectures of the city tend, either to a going beyond and an audacity with no limits in relation to the possible references to the surroundings and its facts (one keeps in abeyance all tradition), or even to a certain nostalgic push toward the former environments of the cities, not perhaps the walls but at least the suburbs and the outskirts. On one hand an architecture of fracture and which is self-sufficient, which is an architecture of an autonomous and temporary city, which one does not need to last for centuries, and whose buildings and their materials are not essentially durable, because they are built and chosen with this idea that they are doomed to be replaced by something else anyway, and very quickly. This architecture, which often ignores its surroundings, its environment, is rather vertical. It gains space from above and it concentrates the activities of industry on a small surface with a favorable relation. Moreover, many cities in the United States are designed on the following model: common place, a large expanse of transient buildings, which is not a suburb but a huge shopping center, and a downtown that mimics the soaring skyscrapers and whose function is most often administrative. The residential areas unravel and scatter between these two sectors. In countries where the countryside still retains an appearance of vocation, the cities promote an extended architecture, by which they will try to join with what remains of this countryside around them, nostalgic towns which become provinces, but alive in their tranquility, and architecture that tries to recompose the already old prestige of the line of perspective. And this architecture will have to be closer to the elements of nature, of earth, stone, wood. It will not be an architecture of glass, plastics, or steel. In any case, in the "sudden" cities or those in total mutation, new street *langages* appear, Creoles of multicultural districts, whose birth is favored by the shock and the conflict between a natural *langage* of young inhabitants and an official *langage* of the place. The difference between the two forms of languages is *quite naturally* the condition for the appearance of Creoles, which at this stage are not yet languages but complex codes of complicity, and which only function in the worlds of these cities, where contacts are multiplied day after day. The Creoles of the Caribbean passed from the Plantation to the villages and then to the cities, according to Faulkner's intuition, before being practiced by all the speakers of each of the societies concerned. In the countrysides of the world, dialects are maintained, the language or languages change very slowly, while in the cities, language is recreated every day. The dialects are slow and stubborn, they last, the Creoles are like lightning and perhaps fragile, as much as the cities and the language codes which constantly change there. Creole languages slow down the rhythm of their changes and their exchanges, as their linguistic solidifying (of the methodical fixation of their lexicons and their syntaxes, where this has been possible) and, moreover, the creolizations that have taken place between the dozens of languages which cover a territory, as in certain parts of Africa, eventuate in an impressive rhizome, made of inextricable exchanges. All these views and conditions, even if they are far away from us, influence the way in which we approach our particular literatures and link them to the balance of the world. Cities and countrysides give rhythm to these movements. There arises from cities a sort of vibration, an energy that consumes itself endlessly, and whose architectural forms also influence our means of expressions. The sudden cities, and the cities that change so breathtakingly, and the cities that shoot up, do so according to a squared, let's say cubic architecture. We see it immediately as such. The cities that stretch toward something else, the countryside or the dream of Relation, suggested by the desire for perspective, are most often of an architecture that we might call rounded. Brasilia mixes the two, thanks to Mr. Niemeyer and the drive to fuse with the Brazilian country. New York uses very few rounded shapes, the curves and the arches of its great *bridges thrust into space* like dizzying spirals that make no circular shape, the image and sum lot of that which remains. In European cities like Paris, rounded shapes are by contrast very present, the cupolas, the arches of the bridges that do not thrust upwards but *dive into the river's water*, the domes, the sinuous streets. In the disaster of most of the underdeveloped countries in the world, countrysides are most often tetanized, reduced to their very skeleton, droughts, dust, floods, epidemics, famines, only the lively decorations of the homes still light up there, and the cities have never had the chance to represent there the aspirations of their inhabitants, traditions are there jammed, these cities are quite simply eaten up by the dismembered chaos of the shantytowns, and the architecture there is characterized first and above all by a genius for bricolage and an art of invention in the detail and scattering, and which perhaps constitutes a style. All of that influences us, even when we have never been to these places. For example, our poetics could be carried by thrusts and struck by a sharp structure, or tempted by diverted routes and unseen sinuosities, or engaged in the lightning inventions of a practice of the real made up of little things and diversions of meanings. Aesthetics move toward the Whole-World, and even if they confine themselves to each one of us, it is a marvel, at the *cohée* it has opened in its sea and in the Rock that one day it encircled. We, we, extreme density, multiple meaning, unavoidable extensions, bending with all the winds that keep us standing.

Acknowledgement

Part of the work for this book was done while I was a Fellow at the National Humanities Center (2020–21). I hereby record my gratitude to the N.H.C.

MM

Printed and bound by CPI Group (UK) Ltd, Croydon, CR0 4YY

14/04/2025

14656919-0001